RYA Rigging Handbook
for Cruisers

by Allan Barwell

© Allan Barwell. First Published 2013

The Royal Yachting Association
RYA House, Ensign Way, Hamble,
Southampton SO31 4YA

Tel: 0844 556 9555 **Fax:** 0844 556 9516
E-mail: publications@rya.org.uk
Web: www.rya.org.uk
Follow us on Twitter @RYAPublications
ISBN: 9781906435509
RYA Order Code: G86

Totally Chlorine Sustainable
Free Forests

D1157291

Edited by: Andrew Simpson
Cover Design: Pete Galvin
Illustrations: Steve Lucas and Andrew Simpson
Typeset: KJS
Proofreading and indexing: Alan Thatcher
Printed in China through World Print

Contents

Introduction

To take a yacht to sea you should have at least a working knowledge of a wide range of skills. You must be a bit of a carpenter, engineer, electrician, cook, navigator and – most importantly – have the seamanship skills necessary to keep you safe. Then, of course, there's the rigging – portrayed by many as something of a black art.

Yet, compared with bygone years, today's rigs are relatively simple. They are made up of superb modern materials. Masts are of aluminium alloys. Synthetic rope is now strong, durable, easy to handle and splice, and comes in many colours to make identification easy. The standing rigging is largely of top-quality rustproof wire, as are the rigging screws and end fittings, which are swaged or fitted by hand. Given the right information, it couldn't be easier.

So, it's my intention to help you with the practicalities and give you the knowledge needed to put yacht rigs together and then maintain them so they remain secure.

Even if you never do the work yourself, the insight will bring you confidence and peace of mind.

Allan Barwell

Foreword

Replacing, maintaining and upgrading ropes can bring many benefits including greater strength, improved safety, lighter weight, better grip, lower stretch, comfortable handling, a longer working life... the list goes on.

It's worth having an idea of the material properties and constructional benefits associated with the different types of rope listed in this book. We often see production yachts with below-spec rope packages designed at a price rather than usability. Using these off-spec ropes becomes a chore or concern to the crew that they may break or jam in sheathes, slip on winches or fail without warning. With a little knowledge a couple of simple changes can make cruising all the more enjoyable.

This book will give you all the knowledge and confidence you need to replace lines on board and make upgrades to specific applications. As well as running rigging this book will give you an insight into standing rigging use, inspection and replacement.

Paul Dyer
Technical Manager
Marlow Ropes

1 | How rigs developed – a brief history

Leisure sailing as we know it today was very different 150 years ago. Then it was mainly commercial sailing boats along with a few private yachts used by the wealthy for pleasure. The Fastnet Race started in 1925 and the competitors would all have been the gentry and well-heeled businessmen from Europe and America.

Due to the different materials used, everything had to be handcrafted and manhandled by a large crew. The whole sailing experience was not what it is today.

At the turn of the 1900s yacht rigs started to develop from those used by commercial fishing boats, such as the smacks, bawleys and sailing barges that once plied our coasts. All of these were gaff rigged and most of the spars were built from wood – spruce being the most usual choice. The standing rigging was of (non-stainless) steel wire and all the running rigging was made from natural fibres such as:

- **Hemp**, a very strong rope whose fibres come, unsurprisingly, from the hemp plant, (cannabis sativa – not to be confused with the variety that produces marijuana!) which was very good for halyards and sheets. Italian hemp was reputedly the strongest and didn't become hard when wet. When tarred it was the best rope for running rigging.

- **Manila**, which comes from plantain (a type of banana) leaf fibres. Although not as strong as hemp, it's much more rot-resistant, and was used a great deal on yachts for mooring and anchor lines.

- **Sisal**, another hard fibre derived from leaves – the agave or aloe, grown in Kenya or Mexico's Yucatan region – but it has about 20 per cent less strength than manila.

- **Coir**, a red-coloured fibre of coconut husks and palm fibre. It floats, it's light and elastic but it lacks strength. It's still used today as tug fender or barge ropes.

- **Cotton**, which was also used. It's very smooth, white, but not as strong as hemp or manila. It was used for smart effects – gangway guard lines, for example – and made excellent dinghy sheets.

Of course, the problem with all these natural-fibre ropes was that they degraded rapidly. Even if they were looked after really well you could expect no more than three or four seasons from them – not like today when most sailors look for several from their running rigging and mooring lines.

And then there were the spars. Making them was a time-consuming business. First, the timber had to be fashioned. Then a blacksmith would make all the metalwork used on spars and deck fittings. He would manufacture mast bands, cranse irons, chain plates, goosenecks and block bindings. An expensive yacht would have the fittings in bronze – poorer sailors opted for iron or steel.

Modern Materials

SPARS

The 1950s saw the advent of extruded aluminium for masts, booms and spinnaker poles. Compared to their wooden predecessors, these offered greater strength for less weight aloft and were also relatively easy to assemble. Over the years that have elapsed since, they have proved to be extremely durable.

WIRES AND FITTINGS

At about the same time, stainless steel wire was replacing the older rust-prone galvanised plough steel that had needed so much work to maintain. Also, such items as shackles, rigging screws and chain plates – previously produced in iron or steel – were now utilising longer-lasting materials such as stainless steel and bronze.

As for terminals, whereas all wire and rope splicing was once done by hand by seamen wielding marlinspikes, with modern materials and the equipment available today we can now use machines to attach end fittings to wire. Alternatively, we might make use of one of the patented self-fit devices such as Norseman® or Sta-Lok® terminals that can be attached using nothing more than simple hand tools (see page 14).

ROPES

Developments in spar technology have been matched by the emergence of synthetic ropes. We shall be dealing with the various forms of rope construction and how to splice them later in chapter 8, but for now let's stick with the materials.

Polyester: This is by far the most common rope material used today, respected for its strength and general utility. It has good resistance to salt and sunlight, is easy to handle and offers good value for money. However, it stretches more than some more exotic fibres, though it can be 'pre-stretched' to improve this characteristic. Many yachts use nothing else for their running rigging.

For those that want higher performance – racing boats, for instance – there are some more expensive options...

Modern ropes come in a variety of fibres, construction and colours

Vectran®: A liquid-crystal polymer (LCP), which, weight for weight, is five times stronger than steel and 10 times stronger than aluminium. It has zero 'creep' – meaning that it doesn't elongate under constant loads. Unfortunately, its UV resistance isn't good (though is said to level out over time) so Vectran ropes almost invariably come with a braided polyester overcoat that also gives protection against abrasion.

HMPE (High Modulus Polyethylene): Marketed under the brand names Spectra® and Dyneema®, these have similar properties to Vectran as well as a very good strength-to-weight ratio. HMPEs have good UV resistance and are often used unsheathed. Commonly used for halyards, guys and sheets – particularly on racing boats, for instance – there are some more expensive options...

Aramids: A high-modulus polyamide better known under the trade names Kevlar®, Twaron® or Technora®. Very strong with a high melting point. Used mainly for abseiling, where friction can melt other ropes. Not common on boats.

PBO: The acronym for *poly(p-phenylene-2,6-benzobisoxazole)*, also known by its trade name 'Zylon®'. This is one of the strongest of today's fibres. Its properties are equal to or better than steel, but it is very much lighter. PBO delivers a no-stretch performance and is ideal on racing yachts, for spinnaker guys, genoa sheets – even for standing rigging. Because of its strength and extremely light weight, halyards and stays can be made in a smaller gauge than the equivalent wire. The only problem is its very high price.

PBO itself is very vulnerable to sunlight, so must be protected with a polyester cover.

Although hardly ever used for yacht rigging, a couple of other rope types deserve a mention because they are commonly used for other tasks on a boat.

Polypropylene: Something of a favourite with dinghy sailors, polypropylene ropes are inexpensive, strong and so light that they float. Common uses on larger boats are for heaving lines and lifebuoy tethers.

Nylon: Because of its stretchiness, nylon is the first choice for anchor warps, mooring lines and towing lines. Nylon has great strength and abrasion qualities and is very good at absorbing shock loads. However, it is slightly absorbent, which can carry salt and dirt into the fibres. It gathers weight with age and has a tendency to become stiff and harder to handle.

2 | Rigs and their elements

Types of Rig

Figure 2:1: Masthead sloop

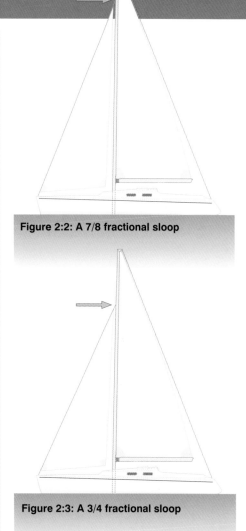

Figure 2:2: A 7/8 fractional sloop

Figure 2:3: A 3/4 fractional sloop

Masthead sloop: This single-masted rig is by far the most popular – particularly for smaller sailboats. It is identifiable by the fact that the backstay and forestay intersect at the masthead.

Economical to make and simple to sail, this is a very reliable rig, both for families and those who sail shorthanded.

Fractional sloop: If your preference is for greater speed and performance – perhaps for club racing – the fractional sloop offers more tuning options. With this type the forestay is attached at a point below the masthead. This means that mast bend can be varied by varying the tension on the backstay to make the belly of the mainsail

flatter or fuller. You will find most fractional sloops will have a tapered top-mast section to make this form of tuning easier.

Fractional rigs are further defined by the point at which the forestay attaches to the mast. For instance, Figure 2:2 shows a 'seven-eighths fractional' rig and Figure 2:3

Staysail

Figure 2:4: Modern cutter

Figure 2:5: Traditional gaff cutter

a 'three-quarters fractional' rig – the reason for these phrases hopefully being obvious.

This type of rig usually calls for running backstays and possibly check stays. Running backstays are there to add extra tension to the forestay while the check stays' job is to support the unstayed mid-sections of the mast, thereby preventing the mast 'panting' in strong wind conditions.

Cutter: This is basically a masthead sloop with a second, inner forestay (Figure 2:4). Usually the mast is stepped slightly further aft to provide space for this arrangement. Instead of a single headsail, cutters generally carry a staysail on the inner forestay and a genoa or 'yankee' on the forestay. Dividing the headsails in this way makes the rig lighter to handle. However, tacking them can sometimes be problematic because big genoas tend to get caught up on the inner forestay as you go about. Cutter rigs are very popular on cruising yachts and also on gaff-rigged boats, as shown in Figure 2:5.

A variation on this rig has a removable inner forestay, which allows a boat to be either a cutter or sloop.

Ketch: A two-masted rig where the aftmost mast – the 'mizzen' mast – is shorter than the main mast. This is a popular rig for larger yachts – particularly those with small crews – because you can divide your sail area into manageable proportions.

However, the extra complexity of having two masts and two sets of rigging does add to the costs. Smaller ketches have declined in popularity, partly due to the development of much better sail-handling deck gear.

Figure 2:6: Ketch

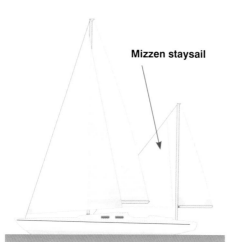

Mizzen staysail

Figure 2:7: Yawl

Ketches are very good off the wind and downwind where, in common with yawls, you can carry extra sails such as mizzen staysails and mizzen spinnakers.

Mizzen staysails are very easy to set, fly on two-masted rigs and are very useful when the wind is on or aft of the beam. The sail's head goes to the top of the mizzen mast with the tack normally attached to the windward side of the deck to windward of the main mast. The clew is sheeted, usually to the end of the mizzen boom, being controlled by the mizzen sheet. A terrific sail for reaching or running.

Yawl: This rig also has a mizzen, though of smaller proportions than a ketch and mounted aft of the rudder stock (Figure 2:7). Yawls share many of the characteristics of ketches, including the advantage

that, when anchored in non-tidal waters, the mizzen can be hoisted and sheeted on the centre line so it keeps the boat head-to-wind.

Francis Chichester's *Gypsy Moth IV* and Joshua Slocum's *Spray* are just two examples of famous sailing yawls.

Schooner: A schooner has two or more masts, either of the same height or with the foremast shorter (Figure 2:8). On a two-masted schooner the mainmast carries the greater sail area. This is another rig that gives the opportunity to set lots of sail options.

A schooner's windward ability is not as good as some other rigs but, once the boat is freed off and you're reaching, the generous sail area gives you lots of power and speed.

Perhaps the most famous schooner is *America*, which came to the Solent and won the 100 Guineas Cup (now known as the America's Cup) in 1851.

Gaffers: Gaff rigs are directly descended from those used on working boats well into the 20th century. Their characteristic four-sided sail gives a large area, producing formidable performance off the wind. They are still in popular use by people who enjoy traditional sailing methods.

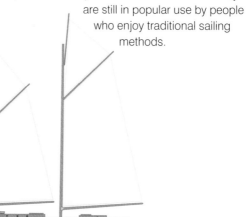

Figure 2:8: Schooner

Masts and Spars

The size of the mast (or masts), the number of spreaders and the details of the standing rigging will be specified by the yacht designer. Masts can have single or multiple sets of spreaders and can be keel-stepped or deck-stepped.

■ Keel-stepped means that the mast passes through the cabin top or deck, where it rests at the bottom of the boat over the keel area. This is a very strong arrangement as there are no downward forces acting upon the deck or cabin top.

   However, to minimise any leakage, keel-stepped masts will need a flexible mast 'gaiter' at the point where the mast passes through the cabin top or deck. A typical mast gaiter is shown below. The top end is fixed around the mast and its conical shape will be fixed to the deck collar where the mast passes through the deck of the boat. Gaiters can be made of neoprene, Hypalon® or canvas – usually one of the first two since they are relatively unaffected by salt water and sunlight.

   As the modern trend is to fit halyard turning blocks bolted to the deck around the mast, another complication is that the

These tensionable straps resist the upward pull of the turning blocks on deck

deck has to be held down by a tension bar or wire to prevent the halyard tension lifting it.

■ Deck-stepped masts are mounted in a shoe or 'tenon' on the cabin top, with the compression loads taken either by a bulkhead or a mast-support post inside the boat.

   Most smaller yachts have deck-stepped masts because it's a simpler, neater and drier arrangement and doesn't intrude as much into the accommodation.

With keel-stepped masts, waterproof gaiters are used to seal the aperture at deck level

Mast Materials

We have already touched on the development of modern spars, but it might be helpful to expand this subject a little further.

Timber: A wooden mast today would only be seen on a traditional style yacht, whether a genuine classic or a modern replica. The timber of choice for working boats was usually solid pine – basically a tree trunk, cleaned of its branches and simply shaped. The weight of the masts was inevitably quite considerable, even though they were planed down to a taper at the top end.

Section through a typical timber spar. It's easy to appreciate the weight involved

Lighter yachts would probably choose Sitka spruce (and these days Douglas fir). To save weight, their spars are usually hollow, using a variety of construction techniques.

Aluminium: These days this is by far the most widely used material, with masts being made from extruded tubes. One great advantage of this manufacturing technique is that features such as sail tracks and cavities designed to house mast reefing systems can be incorporated into the section – though, of course, this

all adds weight. Most masts made today are anodized – a process that thickens the protective oxide layer – but there is now a preference for painted or powder-coated masts.

Nearly all of a modern mast's fittings are standardised – the head boxes, heel castings, spreader roots, goosenecks, pole fittings, and so on. Fabrication is largely a matter of cutting the extrusion to length and either bolting or riveting the various fittings to it. The shape of the mast is very important. To deal with the loads they will meet in service, masts are designed to be stronger in the fore and aft dimension than they are athwartships.

Carbon fibre: Performance boats are increasingly turning to carbon fibre masts, booms and spinnaker booms. These are very expensive to buy but they do have the advantage of being both strong and light. Despite the virtues they do come with some disadvantages.

Because carbon is a very noble material in the galvanic sense (see page 75), the potential for galvanic corrosion to associated fittings is high.

Booms and Poles

Once again aluminium is the most popular choice for the reasons previously described. Booms can incorporate grooves for boltropes and downhauls and other components both external and internal.

Aluminium spinnaker poles are also popular but the light weight of carbon fibre can be tempting, particularly on larger boats.

The biggest problem that we have is maintaining the inboard and outboard working ends. They normally have stainless steel piston pins with springs and locking and release mechanisms. These are highly susceptible to wear and corrosion because of the necessity of these components to be activated and released with high loadings during use. The problem is exacerbated by the fact that spinnaker poles are often only rarely used so have a tendency to seize up.

See chapter 9 for maintenance recommendations.

Standing Rigging

The difference between standing and running rigging is that standing rigging is permanently fixed at both ends of the wire or rope. Running rigging typically has only one end permanently attached and the other end is free for adjustment. Standing rigging is principally there to support the mast and is divided into 'stays' and 'shrouds'. All stays run fore and aft, while shrouds operate athwartships. On masthead rigs the forestay runs from the top of the mast to the stem head fitting and the backstay runs from the top of the mast to the stern chain plate.

As we've already mentioned, on 'fractional' rigs the forestay doesn't go to the top of the mast. On a 'three-quarter' rig it's attached 75 per cent up the mast and on a 'seven-eighths' at about 87 per cent – for reasons that should be obvious. This produces a higher aspect ratio sailplan (meaning taller and narrower) with a

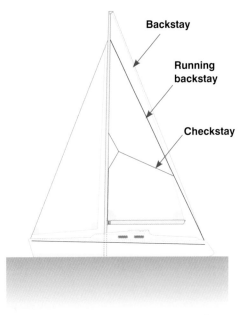

relatively large mainsail and quite a small jib. The mainsail gives most of the power and drive. So the rigging of such a mast will normally include running backstays, which will go to an area on the mast close to where the forestay is fitted to the mast. The running backstay (see above) will control the forestay tension, while the backstay will control mast bend. By tensioning the backstay you can bend the mast, thus slackening the mainsail's leech and flattening the mainsail's belly. Easing the backstay has the opposite effect. So, with a flexible rig you will have excellent sail control.

So much for the stays. For its lateral support a mast relies on the shrouds. The cap shrouds run from high up on the mast to the port and starboard chain plates at deck level, holding the mast upright. The cap shrouds also pass over the ends of spreaders – a single pair for smaller boats, even as many as five or six pairs for the largest rigs. These spreaders put compression into the mast, which is resisted by the lower shrouds (and diagonals on multi-spreader rigs). When properly tuned the mast is supported securely (see page 24).

The main components of
the standing rigging

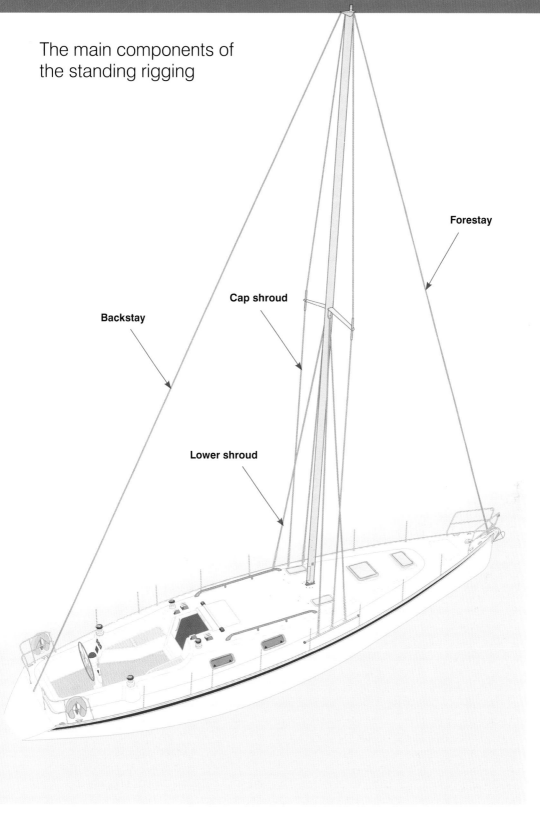

Forestay

Cap shroud

Backstay

Lower shroud

The standing rigging on most cruising yachts is usually made of 1 x 19 stainless steel wire. The construction of the wire calls for 19 wires all of the same diameter. One wire runs up the middle, six wires are wound around the centre wire, and twelve wires are wound in the opposite direction around them – hence 1 x 19.

1 x 19 wire

A variation on the 1 x 19 theme uses shaped strands, thereby compacting more metal – and therefore more strength – into the same overall diameter.

High-performance yachts go a step further and use a solid rod to form their stays and shrouds – an expensive option involving a 'cold heading' process to make the terminations.

Much more on wire types and their relative strengths will be found on page 72.

End fittings: The shroud and stay attachments come in various forms: eyes, forks, tees or stemballs. This is determined by the mast manufacturer. Most modern rigging has swaged terminals, which have proved very reliable and long lasting.

The terminals are fitted by using a roll-swaging machine. The wire is put into the swage terminal and the machine rolls and squeezes the swage terminal onto the wire. Each size of swage terminal is matched to the swaging tools, which is very accurately constructed and incredibly strong.

We can also use self-fitting terminals, of which well-known brands are Norseman®, Sta-lock® and Bluewave®. All the self-fit terminals cover the same range of eyes, forks, tees and studs (see photo below). These fittings are normally more expensive than roller swaging but are very easy to fit. For proper performance you must follow the manufacturers' instructions.

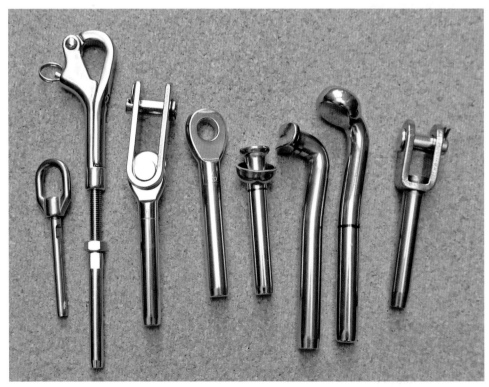

Stainless steel end fittings come in a variety of shapes and sizes

Roll swaging machines are often portable so riggers can work on or at least near the boat

Rigging screws: The rigging is adjusted by means of rigging screws that tension the rig to give the mast its column shape. The materials used to make these fittings are normally of very high-quality stainless steel 316 with chromed bronze barrels for rigging screws. All shroud and stay attachments should have toggles at the lower ends so that the fittings are totally articulated. It is very important that the forestay that is subjected to side loads has toggles at both top and bottom ends.

Shackles: Shackles don't usually form part of the standing rigging but they can sometimes be useful. If shackles are used, once made secure they should be seized with Monel® seizing wire so that they cannot come loose. Only use the best quality shackles, preferably stainless steel, of forged construction from reputable manufacturers.

Rigging Screws

Rigging screws made entirely of stainless steel were once popular and a number are still in service today. If adjusted under load they have a tendency for the barrels and threaded studs to 'gall' together. This is an inadvertent form of friction welding that literally seizes the two parts into one, destroying the threads. Of course, the rigging screw becomes useless. The chromed bronze and stainless steel rigging screws described above don't suffer from this unfortunate problem.

Running Rigging

A boat's running rigging is made up of such things as sheets, guys, halyards, lifts, downhauls and reefing lines – all of which are involved in controlling the sails. All of the ropes shown in the illustration right represent various types of running rigging and are operated by slackening or tightening the particular control.

Although flexible wire rope (usually with a rope 'tail' so it could be used on a standard winch) was once popular for halyards, the vast majority of today's running rigging is made from polyester, which is very strong and reliable and also relatively low in cost. If you want less stretch and greater strength you may need to look at one of the high-performance fibres (Spectra®, Dyneema®) we looked at back on page 6, but for most purposes polyester will probably do.

Most modern forms of rope construction can be satisfactorily spliced, a subject we'll be covering fully in chapter 8. However, it's worth mentioning now that the construction of some ropes makes splicing much more difficult than others.

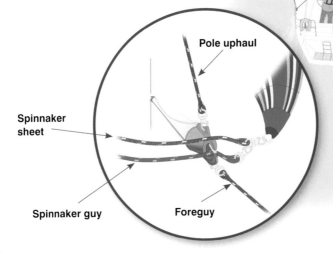

Pole uphaul

Spinnaker sheet

Spinnaker guy

Foreguy

The purpose of the running rigging is to control the sails

3 | Craning masts into position

Craning masts is one of the most crucial operations a boat is subjected to and it must be done with great care, firstly to spare the boat and rig unnecessary damage and, secondly, for the safety of the people engaged in the task.

Stepping Masts

It is usually easier to crane a mast into a yacht with the boat in the water rather than on the hard standing. This is because the crane doesn't have to reach so high – sometimes a serious limitation with very tall masts. Careful preparation will ensure the lift goes smoothly. This means that:

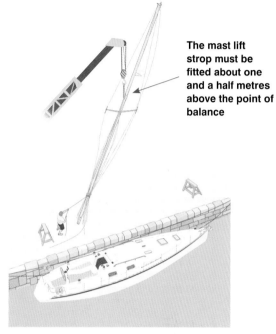

The mast lift strop must be fitted about one and a half metres above the point of balance

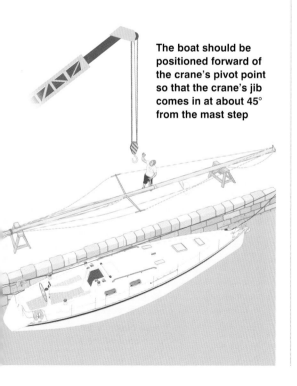

The boat should be positioned forward of the crane's pivot point so that the crane's jib comes in at about 45° from the mast step

■ The boat must be secured very tightly to the pontoon or quayside because, once the mast touches the heel attachment point, it will tend to push the boat either fore, aft or out. The boat should be positioned forward of the crane's pivot point so that the crane's jib comes in at about 45° from the mast step.

■ The mast lift strop must be fitted about one and a half metres above the point of balance. Also, a heel rope should be attached to the lower end of the mast to control the lift and to stop it swinging uncontrollably.

■ All the rigging screws and adjusters must be fully open so that connection can be made easily to the chain plates.

By picking the mast up from the after side, it means that the jib of the crane is free of the mast and the forestay, radar, electronics and rigging does not get tangled on the jib of the crane. From there the procedure should go like this:

1. The mast is lifted and swung forward over the boat's stern to the point where you can connect the forestay by inserting the clevis pin and split pin. Having done that, the mast should now be engaged in its step.

2. Jibbing the crane aft of this will bring the mast upright and allow you to connect the cap shrouds and aft lowers with their clevis pins. Once connected this will stop the mast falling forward.

Once the mast is stepped, check over carefully that all clevis pins are secure with split pins open to about 20°–25°.

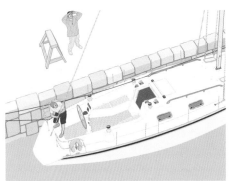

3. Normally the backstay is connected once the mast lift is taken away and the jib of the crane removed out of the way. Connecting the backstay will then make the mast totally secure. If necessary, halyards can also be used to secure the mast.

WARNING!
Remember that the wind strength will be greater at the masthead than it is at deck level. Never underestimate the effects it can have on any mast-lift operation.

Unstepping Masts

As before, the boat should be secured alongside in exactly the same position relative to the crane as recommended for stepping the mast. The procedure is very much the reverse of stepping the mast, but first you must complete the following preparations.

Step 1: Before unstepping your mast you must undo all the electrics and electronic cables so that they are free to come through the deck. You need to remove the mainsail from the mast, plus the boom and all halyards that go through deck turning lead blocks running back to the cockpit.

It will pay first to mark the rigging screws (with tape) at their current settings so that, when you slacken, you get back near to your previous tensions when the mast is re-stepped.

It's also helpful to pull the split pins away on the chain plate connection – and then put half a split pin back in the clevis pin so that it's quicker to pull out once the mast is ready to lift.

Step 2: On small yachts we use a strop around the mast – on single-spreader rigs, usually just below the spreaders. On larger yachts with multiple spreaders it will require someone in a bosun's chair (see page 26 for guidance on how to do this safely) to go up the mast and fit a strop a metre or so above the point of balance. There should also be a heel rope at the base of the mast and another at the lower end of any roller-reefing gear. A hand should be assigned to each heel rope.

Once you are ready, the crane can take the weight of the mast and the stays and shrouds released. Since the jib comes in from about 45° from astern, it's kept well clear of such fragile items as the roller-reefing or a mast-mounted radar.

In either case, great care must be taken to ensure any roller-reefing gear is kept as straight as possible to prevent damage.

Step 3: Once the mast is on the ground it's sensible to remove aerials, wind instruments and bulbs to protect them from damage (and theft). Then, if possible, the mast should be laid on trestles, keeping it clear of the ground and ensuring that the mast lies as straight as possible.

Keel-stepped Masts

When lifting any mast, keel-stepped or otherwise, the way that the mast is lifted and controlled is very important. Damage can occur to the interior structure – bulkheads being an obvious example – if the heel of the mast is allowed to come into contact as the mast is lifted. With keel-stepped masts the heel rope should be attached approximately two feet above the deck.

Winter Storage

If you are unstepping your mast to store for the winter it should be stored on a level rack. Since the roller reefing is probably longer than the mast, it should be disconnected so that it can protrude beyond the masthead. That way the heavier drum end can be lashed to the foot of the mast to give it plenty of support.

Ideally, you should remove all standing rigging and possibly even the halyards, replacing these with messengers. Also, wash the mast thoroughly with soapy water and then cover in polythene sheeting. This will protect it from winter weather, dirt and grime. Better still, you can store it inside.

All electrical terminals should be protected by enclosing them in plastic bags, taped in place to keep out as much water as possible. A small hole at the lowest point of each bag can help any leakage drain away.

Having the mast on the ground will give you ample time to inspect and make any necessary repairs or improvements over the winter period.

4 Dressing and rigging a new mast

When faced with a new mast, the first task is to fit all the equipment to it. This could include the halyards, winches, spreaders, electrics, wind instruments, VHF aerial, navigation lights and radar. It often helps to remove the heel fitting to gain access to internal conduits.

New masts normally come with 'messengers' – lengths of light line already shaped to pull new ropes or electrical cable into position. However, this may not always be so, so you may need to use a 'mouse' – either a length of stiff wire or an electrician's mouse, which you can obtain from your local electrical trade supplier.

Winches, cleats and jammers can be fitted easily by using pop rivets (also known as 'blind' rivets) or machine screws. Pop rivets are widely used and should be made of 'Monel®', an alloy of copper and nickel, which is much stronger than the more common aluminium rivets and less likely to

When fittings are attached to a mast you must be aware of dissimilar metals that could suffer galvanic corrosion (see page 75). So you will have to use zinc chromate paste or a plastic isolation pad between surfaces to avoid any aluminium oxide forming due to galvanic action.

cause corrosion. Most chandlers stock them.

Monel rivets require heavy-duty rivet guns like these shown here

Drilling and Tapping

Drilling and tapping is the process of introducing a screw thread into solid metal – usually aluminium in our case. The process goes like this:

■ A 'pilot hole' is drilled, somewhat smaller than the diameter of the fastening – usually a machine screw. For example, tapping an aluminium 5mm thread would require a 4mm hole. See 'Tapping guide for aluminium' on page 73.

■ For thin-walled material, as found on mast extrusions and winch pads, a tapered tap is ideal. A 'cutting compound' must be used to lubricate the tap as it is carefully wound in. Once the thread is cut, the lubricant must be cleaned away, ready to receive the fastening.

■ When attaching fittings, a useful precaution is to apply a few drops of thread-locking solution to all tapped threads.

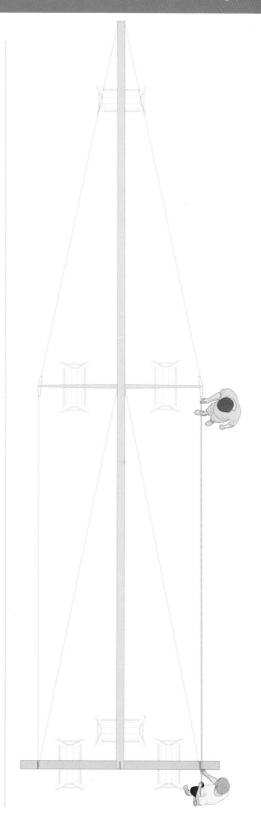

Warning!

Some yachtsmen use self-tapping stainless screws, but this is not recommended. They tend to break or snarl and they also have sharp pointed ends that can damage halyards flapping around inside the mast.

As for strength, 6.4mm Monel® rivets will have a shearing breaking strain around 700 kilos. They are fitted with a heavy duty rivet gun. A 4.8mm rivet will have a breaking strain of about 400 kilos and can be set with a smaller DIY-type rivet gun.

When stainless steel machine screws are used we normally drill and tap into the aluminium.

Once this preparatory task is done, you can turn to the standing rigging, the accurate measurement of which will first entail what's known as 'spanning off the mast'.

We start with the shrouds.

Spanning the Cap Shrouds

When confronted with a brand-new installation, it would be tempting to look at the sailplan drawing and assume that all the dimensions were accurately portrayed. You might think that you could simply measure off the stays and shrouds from the drawing and start cutting the wire to length.

This would be a mistake. There are too many variables that could make theory differ from reality and could lead you to either underestimate or overestimate the lengths. Bearing in mind that the amount of 'travel' on a rigging screw is only a matter of very few inches, there isn't much room for error. Spanning is best done with the mast laid out on trestles. The spreaders should be fitted.

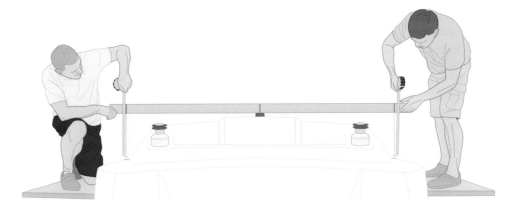

1. Determine where the foot of the mast will rest and, at that level, lay a straight wooden beam athwartships (at 90° to the centreline) and as horizontal as possible.

2. With masking tape, mark the distance outboard (from the centreline) to the attachment point of the appropriate chain plate. Use the centre of the holes on both sides as the terminal points. Next, measure the vertical distances below the beam to the centre of the holes (again, do both sides). There may be slight differences in the vertical measurements. Add them together and divide by two to get the average.

3. Now take the beam to the foot of the mast and square it up in order to take measurements from the cap shroud tangs at the top of the mast, around the ends of the spreaders and down to the top of the beam. Again, there might be slight differences and these should be averaged as described above.

4. Now all that remains is to make up the cap shrouds, using either a swaging machine or self-fit fittings. Don't forget to make allowances for the lengths of the terminals plus rigging screws, which should be extended to three-quarter length.

Now for the stays and lower shrouds.

Step 1 The lower shrouds, backstay and intermediates are cut over length. They will be trimmed over-length with the mast standing, then swaged or fitted with Norseman® or Sta-lok® terminals. You will also need a 'temporary' forestay, for the purpose as described on the opposite page.

Step 2 For temporary support of the mast when stepped, you will need extra lines: two forward, two aft, fitted around the spreader area. The main, topping lift, and foresail halyards will also come in useful.

Step 3 Once the mast is stepped, the two cap shrouds will give support to the mast athwartships and you can attach your steadying lines and halyards so they will secure the mast in a fore-and-aft direction. The next job is to fit the terminals and rigging screws to the forward and aft lower shrouds. If these are self-fit terminals, adhere strictly to the manufacturer's instructions.

Step 4 Now it's time to set the correct rake, as specified by the designer. This can be achieved by first looking at the boat's waterline to judge whether the yacht is floating on its lines. If it isn't, you will have to allow for any discrepancy in the next stage. Step away from the yacht (hopefully it's alongside!) and use a spirit level and set square to judge the rake and make the adjustments necessary to bring it as closely as possible to the designer's specification. Any minor adjustments can be done later.

Step 5 Once the correct rake has been established, we know the length of the temporary forestay (as described in the panel below) so just add the extension measurement point, which will give you an accurate forestay length. We can now make up the permanent forestay, complete with roller-reefing if fitted.

Step 6 The next task is to replace the temporary forestay with the permanent one. To do this, you will need to climb the mast, and the safest way to do this is in a bosun's chair (see page 26).

Step 7 Your rig is now ready to set up. When tightening or adjusting rigging screws – both old or new – first lubricate the threads with petroleum jelly (Vaseline) or Teflon® grease. Don't use any form of mineral oil or grease since these can stain. Then, once the rig is set up, wipe away any residues so there's nothing left behind that could stain sails or clothing.

Double-spreader Rigs

So far we've been talking about single-spreader rigs but many boats – particularly larger ones – have multi-spreader rigs, anywhere from two pairs to several. These rigs can be divided into two separate categories, all related to the nature of the cap shrouds:

■ Continuous rigging means that the cap shrouds run from the masthead all the way down to the chain plate at deck level – in other words 'continuously'. Sometimes even the intermediates also run from the root of the upper spreader, through the end of the lower spreader, then down to the deck.

The advantages are that this arrangement is cheaper and simpler to fit. However, there is more windage and clumsier chain plates.

■ Discontinuous rigging means that the cap shrouds and intermediates terminate at the end of the lower spreaders with the load being transferred to the deck by stronger and larger lower cap shrouds.

The advantages lie in weight and windage but costs are higher.

Determining the Forestay Length

With the mast upright, don't think you can use a long tape measure to determine the lengths of the various rigging elements. Even in the slightest breeze the tape will vibrate and flutter enough to make precise measurements impossible.

Instead, I take an old piece of rigging wire (riggers accumulate lots of it – you may be able to scrounge some!) and make it up to a length – a known length – approximately equal to that of a deck-stepped mast (masthead to deck) with an eye in both ends. One end is attached to the masthead tang and the other will be secured with a lashing to the stemhead fitting. Once the mast rake has been set up as specified by the designer, the forestay length can be measured accurately simply by adding the distance from the lower eye to the forestay tang to the known length of your temporary forestay. You can now build the headsail roller-reefing gear (in accordance with the manufacturer's instructions) or complete the 'real' forestay, confident that you know its length precisely.

5 Tuning the rig

Now that we have the mast in the boat we can set about the tuning of the rigging. For tools you will need:

- Adjustable spanners – one to hold the top of the rigging screw while the barrel is rotated, and another to fit the barrel. Always use quality spanners, which are in good condition. Rusty tools will contaminate the rigging, probably leaving a rust residue.

Always use good quality spanners to adjust the rigging screws

- A steel rule (about 30cm long) to ensure that the rigging screws are all tensioned equally.
- A bosun's chair (see page 26) to ascend the mast.

From there on, the sequence goes like this:

1. Check that you have the correct mast rake, then tighten the backstay firmly.

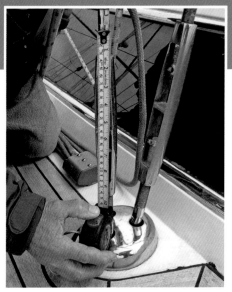

Make sure that the rigging screw threads are equal top and bottom

2. Next, turn to the cap shrouds and tighten these. Make sure that the rigging screw threads are equal top and bottom and also port and starboard.

3. At this point you should ensure that the masthead is on the centreline. This is best done when the mast is on the ground by making sure that the cap shrouds are exactly the same length overall – meaning the combined length of the wire and rigging screws is the same. It then follows that, if the rigging screws are equally tensioned once the mast is standing, the masthead must be on the centreline.

   So now you have both the foot and head of the mast on the centreline but the length in between is almost certainly bowed. To bring it back into column, the lower shrouds must be adjusted – and here it helps to peer up the mainsail track where any slight deviation will be most obvious.

On double-spreader rigs the later straightness of the mast is determined by adjusting D1 and D2

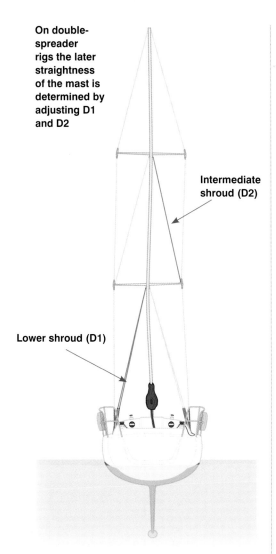

Intermediate shroud (D2)

Lower shroud (D1)

The purpose of pre-bend is to enhance the shape of the mainsail

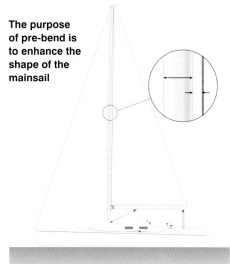

5. Generally, the rigging should be tensioned to about 20 per cent of the wire's breaking strain – though this is difficult to determine without specialised equipment. As a rule-of-thumb, a cap shroud should feel firm when pulled sideways.

6. The final tuning should be done with the boat sailing to windward in flat water in about a F4–5 wind. Look up the mast to see how straight it is both fore-and-aft and laterally. If the top of the mast falls away to leeward, that will tell you that the cap shrouds need to be tensioned. If the middle of the mast falls away it will require the lowers to be tensioned. This must be done on both tacks and noted so that when you return to harbour you can…

7. …readjust the shrouds. Some people will tell you that you should set up the leeward shroud under sail when it is slack but I think that this is a very imprecise method and can easily over-tension your rig.

8. Once your rigging has been readjusted you should repeat the same test as before to make sure that the mast is still in column on both tacks.

4. Masts are usually tuned so they bow forwards slightly in the middle. This is called 'pre-bend' and is intended to improve mainsail shape. Getting the correct pre-bend is achieved by adjusting the forward lower shrouds or the baby stay. Mast bend on swept spreader-rigs is induced by the forward compression of the spreaders and is constrained by intermediate and lower shroud tensions. It's a little trickier to get right – a subject we'll deal with shortly.

How to use a Bosun's Chair Safely

The safest way to climb a mast is in a bosun's chair.

The climber will be pulled up the mast on a halyard, preferably with another halyard used as a safety back-up. For the primary line the main halyard is usually the obvious choice, firstly because it passes through the masthead, which means that security isn't reliant on the strength of the sheave and, secondly, it usually leads conveniently to a powerful winch.

- The primary line should be tied to the chair's attachment point with a bowline or a conventional shackle. Never rely on a snapshackle. The back-up line is usually the spinnaker halyard.
- If using a back-up line you need at least two crew on deck to handle the halyards (plus one more to tail the main halyard if the winch isn't self-tailing).
- Self-tailers should only be used in self-tailing mode if there are also rope clutches as back-ups.

Going up...

GOLDEN RULE 1: While he's actually winching, the principal winchman should keep his eyes on the winch, not the climber. This will avoid the chance of any riding turns or other foul-ups.

GOLDEN RULE 2: If the halyard winches are on the mast, send the tools up in a bucket once the climber is in place. To have, say, a cordless drill fall from the bosun's chair onto the wincher standing below could be bad news for everyone concerned – not least for the climber who could follow it to the deck if said wincher became distracted. The alternative is to have each tool attached with a lanyard to the chair, so nothing can be dropped from a height.

Which takes us to...

GOLDEN RULE 3: Once the halyards are secured, stand clear of the mast while work is in progress.

An alternative to the back-up line is for the climber to use a mountaineering 'ascender' (a type of jamming cleat) attached to the chair via a short rope strop and run up a spare halyard that has been set up fairly tight by tensioning it with a winch. The spinnaker halyard is a strong candidate for this role.

...and down again.

Again, as you lower the climber, the wincher's eyes should be on the drum, not up the mast. Riding turns are more common when easing than when hauling. And...

GOLDEN RULE 4: The winchers must ease the halyards hand-over-hand, instead of allowing the rope to slip through their fingers. This is in case something sharp – a piece of glass or wire, for instance – may have become caught in the rope, the sudden pain of which might cause a startled wincher to release his or her grip.

Swept-spreader Rigs

Swept-spreader rigs are becoming increasingly popular, largely because of their simplicity and economy. Basically, you need fewer materials to hold the mast up. Mast design has adapted to suit the new fashion. As with more traditional rigs, the swept-spreader type can be either masthead or fractional, having single or multiple spreaders. The modern trend is to fit almost full-width spreaders.

With fewer shrouds, it is inevitable that more load is placed on those that are left. Fractional swept-spreader rigs are very dependant on cap shroud tension to keep the forestay taut – an important issue for cruising yachts with heavy roller reefing systems.

Tuning Single Swept-spreader Rigs

When adjusting masts with swept-spreaders, it's important to understand that the spreaders induce a forward force into the mast, so contribute to the mast's shape and column, both side-to-side and fore-and-aft. This makes them a little more time-consuming to tune.

■ First, tension the forestay, ensuring that the mast rake is correct.

■ Next, tension the backstay quite firmly.

■ Now it's time to tension the cap shrouds. As described on page 24, for 'normal' squared-off spreaders, the cap shrouds must be exactly the same length to ensure that the masthead is on the centreline. From this point on, any adjustments to the cap shroud rigging's screws must be identical on both sides.

■ If the mast has both forward and aft lower shrouds, tension the forward lowers first.

Then look up the after side of the mast to make sure the mast is 'in column' – in other words the track is straight. There should also be some pre-bend in the mast.

■ Now to adjust the aft lowers, but do not over-tension since this will pull the pre-bend out of the mast.

■ Lastly, check the forestay tension by hand – making sure there is very little sag in the roller-reefing – before going aft and tightening the backstay.

■ Later, with the boat under sail, check that the mast is still in column and, on both port and starboard tacks, note whether the top or middle part of the mast falls away to leeward. If the first is observed, the cap shrouds should be tightened; if the middle falls away, the aft lowers should be tightened. The object of this is to keep the mast in column on all points of sail.

NOTE: Any adjustments must be made identically on each side of the boat. Some people advise making the adjustments at sea but my preference is to wait until the sail is down and there are no wind loads on the rig.

Tuning Multi-spreader Fractional Rigs

These are tuned in a similar way to single-spreader rigs but you may need the use of a bosun's chair to go up to the lower spreaders to adjust the intermediates (D2).

■ Follow the sequence in the same way as before, forestay, backstay, and cap shrouds.

■ Multi-spreader fractional rigs don't usually have forward lowers so the next task is the aft lowers (D1). Tension these equally to pull the mast back into column. Look up the mast frequently to check that the mast stays straight in the athwartships axis.

■ Next we should adjust the aft lowers. Tighten them equally and firmly, making sure you don't take out the pre-bend.

■ The next task is the intermediates. On continuous rigging, these can be adjusted from deck level but, if discontinuous, you will need a bosun's chair to go up the lower spreaders. Either way, these must be adjusted – again equally. If you are at the first spreaders, you obviously need someone on deck looking up the mast to check that the track is true and straight. Be careful not to over-tighten any intermediates, since this will introduce a tendency for the upper spans of the mast to fall to leeward.

Again, the rig should be checked under sail, making any further adjustments that may be necessary.

Finally…

Once you are satisfied that the mast is set up correctly you can then pin and tape all rigging screws. On a new installation on a new boat you will find that the shroud tensions will tend to slacken off a little once the boat has been sailed. This is due to stretch in the wire, some movement in the chain plates, and the mast step bedding down under the compression load. So once the boat has been sailed a few times (in strongish weather) it will be necessary to tighten and make minor adjustments to the standing rigging.

Tip The Proper Way to set Split Pins

For a mast with stainless steel tangs and clevis pin connections, the split pin should be between the tang and the mast – that's to say, inboard. This also applies to backstay fittings.

In most cases, split pins don't need to be opened more than 25° (see Figure 1). However, on the forestay I prefer to open the split pin aircraft-style so the legs of the split pin wrap right around the clevis pin (see Figure 2). Once, sailing across the Atlantic to Antigua, I climbed the mast and found all spilt pins were in place and secure. After 19 days at sea, in Antigua I climbed the mast again to find that the forestay clevis pin had no split pin. This was caused by a wire halyard that had broken the split pin legs, allowing it to fall out!

To avoid injury to the crew, all split pins at deck level need to be protected either with tape or some kind of rigging screw covers.

Figure 1: Split pin opened to 20°

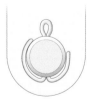

Figure 2: Split pin (wrapped around aircraft-style)

6 | Reefing

In days gone by, yachts would carry a comprehensive sail wardrobe. The headsails alone would include large lightweight genoas for use in light conditions, through to heavier working sails to be set when the wind pipes up, down to storm jibs for when things get seriously stormy. By contrast, today the most common practice is to have sails that can be furled and unfurled to deal with different wind strengths – all operated from the safety of the cockpit rather than having crew working on the foredeck.

While boats have generally got bigger they are still often manned by smaller crews, such as families and couples. There's no doubt that these mechanical developments have made the task of sail handling much easier but they also bring their problems.

Genoa reefing: Although mainsail reefing systems are gaining ground, the use of headsail roller-reefing has become almost universal for cruising yachts. A typical installation relies on a line wound around a drum, which, when pulled, causes an extruded foil – usually of aluminium – to rotate around the forestay. This simple action winds the headsail around it. Larger units might well be hydraulically or electrically driven.

Simple they might be but, like with all mechanical devices, problems can arise. In order to give their products the best possible chance of working smoothly, most manufacturers give you detailed instructions on setting up their gears correctly. Some of the advice may be specific to a certain gear but general points to watch out for are:

■ It's important for the forestay to be really

Headsail roller-reefing gear

taut to keep the furling extrusion as straight as possible. If there's a lot of slackness, the foil will sag to leeward and become very difficult to turn.

■ To prevent the halyard wrapping around the foil, the halyard swivel must ascend as high as possible on the extrusion. If this isn't practicable, it may be necessary to fit a sheave box into the mast about 20cm down from the mast head (the halyard emerges at a lower point).

> **Tip**
>
> When leaving a boat it's advisable to put a lashing from the sail's tack (on the drum) and make this fast to the pulpit. This means even if the reefing line is released the sail cannot unwind.

Alternatively, a top deflector might be installed.

■ If a sail's luff is a good bit shorter than the headfoil you will need an equalising pennant (typically a short piece of 7 x 19 wire with a Talurit® eye at each end) at the top of the sail so the swivel can travel all the way to the top. Alternatively, you could fit the pennant to the sail's tack, thus lifting the foot. On cruising boats this has the added advantage that it makes it easier to see under the sail when you are in the cockpit.

■ Make sure that spinnaker halyards are kept well away from a rotating headfoil. It's very easy to wind them into the headsail top swivel.

■ Other problems are caused by the reefing line not going onto the drum at the correct angle or without sufficient tension. When you release the furling line, it's important to ease it slowly. To allow it to run freely is to ask for trouble. Riding turns can easily develop, which could jam the furler when it comes to roll the sail in again.

■ When the boat is on a mooring or in a marina make sure you have at least two turns of the genoa sheets around the sail. In windy conditions or if leaving the boat for a while, it also makes sense to put a lashing around the clew so that it cannot get loose and unfurl.

Headsail furling gears are improving all the time, but of course quality is reflected in the price. Some reefing systems have sealed bearings but, as we have found over the years, salt water can enter and the bearings can fail to work properly. Some systems use open bearings – normally Torlon® – that can simply be washed out with fresh water to remove salt crystals.

Further advice is given in our Maintenance chapter starting on page 64.

Clearing a Jammed Reefing System

Jammed roller headsails can occur in two ways. The first is a halyard wrap, which should never occur if the advice on page 29 is followed.

The second is a tangle of the reefing line in its drum at the lower end of the foil. As previously described, this problem usually arises from allowing the reefing line to pay out too fast.

Whatever the cause, the best solution is to run downwind so there's very little load in the sail and the boat is more or less upright. It should then be possible to untangle the line, perhaps with the aid of a marlinspike.

In-mast Mainsail Reefing

Perhaps it was inevitable that roller reefing should be adapted to include mainsails, and over the past few years these have gained in popularity. The first were behind-the-mast retrofits that adapted the existing mast, but today masts are specially extruded so that the mainsail can be furled inside them, more or less completely out of sight.

In-mast main reefing gears require a very flat-cut sail to allow them to be wound into the mast without jamming. It's also important to have the boom at the correct angle so that you have equal tension on both the leech and the foot of the sail. If the leech is too tight then the foot will be saggy and this will bunch up inside the extrusion. Indeed, most problems with in-mast furling systems are caused by the poor construction of the sail or the incorrect boom angle.

Friction can be a problem with in-mast reefing so you should ensure that the outhaul and reefing lines need to have little resistance through the blocks and the deck's fairlead blocks, as this will make sail handling heavy and difficult.

In-mast mainsail reefing is becoming increasingly popular. However, although undoubtedly convenient, mechanical complexity can bring its problems

A boat with a jammed in-mast reefing mainsail limps into port with the main only partially furled. It took over an hour to clear the jam. See 'Tip' below for hints on how to minimise such problems

Clearing an In-mast Reefing System

This is a much more serious problem than a jammed headsail and there is no single or simple answer. On the positive side, at least jams tend to occur towards the bottom of the mast, where there's the greatest volume of sail, so it might be possible to inch it out from just above the boom. If the jam occurs higher up, there's no alternative but to go up the mast in a bosun's chair and lever the sail out with something like a large flat screwdriver.

You may be able partially to snuff the sail by winding the spinnaker halyard around both the mast and sail. The halyard can be extended by tying another line to it. This perhaps will allow you to motor into a sheltered area where your struggles will at least be easier.

Tip

When winding a roller-reefing mainsail in, don't use the normal technique of going head to wind, but keep the wind on the beam so that the sail will wind straight through the sail entry slot without rubbing hard against the aluminium sides to that slot.

If the sail winds in anti-clockwise, the boom should be to port. If the sail winds in clockwise, the reverse is the case.

With halyard tensions, it pays not to over-tighten the halyard as this will cause the top swivel to jam.

In-boom Mainsail Reefing

The idea that the boom should be used for reefing has been around for many years. In the old days we used to roll the sail around a rotating boom – an arrangement that was always a little untidy, caused the boom to droop, and made it difficult to fit a kicking strap.

Since then, boom reefing has become more sophisticated.

One of the big challenges is that the angle between boom and mast is absolutely critical. If this isn't exactly right, the sail will creep along the boom, either forward or back. Some designs have a suspended track or luff groove away from the mast sail track that helps introduce some tolerance in the alignment.

The customary way to drive the in-boom reefer will be a 'line-driver' system, which will have a continuous furling line – an endless loop transferred back to winches operated from the cockpit. On larger yachts they are likely to be driven by hydraulic or electrical systems.

Both in-mast and in-boom reefing allows you to control how much mainsail you have set without leaving the cockpit. But, whereas in-mast reefing leaves the sail's weight aloft at all times, in-boom reefing lowers it as the sail comes down.

Mainsail Slab-reefing Methods

Despite the growing enthusiasm for mechanised reefing systems, there are many sailors who still choose the older tried and tested techniques, which, although less convenient, are undoubtedly simpler and more reliable.

To slab reef a mainsail is basically to put a tuck in it. This gives a generally better shape to the sail than roller reefing, so is almost invariably the first choice on board performance and racing boats.

There are various ways of doing it:

Single clew downhaul, tack to cowhorn: The most common system of a single clew downhaul/outhaul is shown below. A line runs from the end of the boom up to the reefing clew then down to a sheave on the end of the boom. It will then go forward to the goose neck.

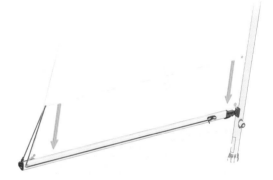

When reefing…
- …first depower the mainsail by letting the boom swing off to the quarter.
- Next, tighten the topping lift to take the weight of the boom. This won't be necessary if you have a solid kicker.
- Then, ease the main halyard to lower the mainsail and allow the first reef tack cringle to be attached to the cowhorn. Once attached, retighten the halyard.
- Now use the reefing line to pull the reef clew cringle down to the boom. If this proves difficult, use the topping lift to raise the boom up to the level of the cringle. It's very important that the reefing line be tight to maintain the foot tension in the reefed sail.

You will be left with the loose 'bunt' hanging down. Traditionally, this would be tidied up with reefing pennants but better methods are described overleaf.

Twin lines led back to cockpit: With the system shown here, both the tack and clew reefing lines go back to the cockpit, as does the main halyard and topping lift.

Jiffy reefing: This is a low-price single-line system, reeved as shown below.

Preparations to reef are as before. From there the sequence goes as follows:

- The reef is taken by simply hauling on the single reef line. Due to the amount of friction inherent in the system, this will probably require a winch.
- Another problem is that the tack tends to come down first, leaving the clew still loose. Topping the boom up to the clew can help.

In my opinion this is a poor alternative to the other options.

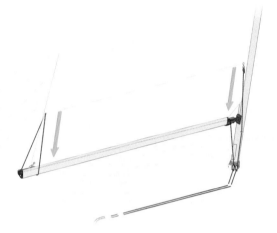

- As before, you tighten the topping lift and depower the sail by easing the mainsheet.
- From the cockpit, release the main halyard enough to pull first the tack then the clew down with their respective reefing lines.
- Finally, retension the halyard and retrim the main.

This is one of the simplest and most reliable systems, a great favourite of many offshore sailors.

Single line with balance block in boom: This is a twin-line system that, in practice, behaves like a single line-system and is operated in very much the same way. The use of blocks – usually inside the boom – minimises friction and ensures that tack and clew are pulled into position evenly.

However, the length of the boom and the height of the cringles usually means that only two reefs are possible, so a third method – usually a single clew line, must be rigged for very heavy conditions.

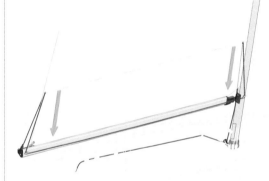

> **Tip**
> With slab-reefing mainsails in heavy weather, it usually helps to have the boom off the leeward quarter so that the sail is not powered up. You can then use the topping lift to lift the boom upwards towards the new clew – usually an easier task than pulling the sail down to the boom.

Lazy Jacks and Sail Packs

On most yachts with conventional mainsails, the best way of containing the mainsail as it is lowered is to fit lazy jacks, which stop the sail from blowing away off the boom. This system is very simple as can be seen below.

The arrangement I prefer is to have the lazy jack secured to an eye on the mast and the tension line coming down to the boom with a jamming cleat. This stops lines that come down the mast from flapping.

Some sailmakers now also favour what are known as sail pack systems. These are like canvas hammocks attached to the boom on both sides, with the lazy jacks fitted to the canvas in such a way as to form a bag. Once the sail has been lowered into the bag you can zip it up, thereby containing the sail in a very tidy fashion.

When raising the mainsail you must make sure that the sail battens and head board clear the lazy jacks. Ease the mainsheet and allow the sail to flog lightly. It should then pass clearly up through the lazy jack system. Alternatively, the lazy jacks can be loosened and walked forward to the mast, where they can be hooked around a spare cleat. Lowering the sail it is much easier, passing down through the lazy jacks without a hitch.

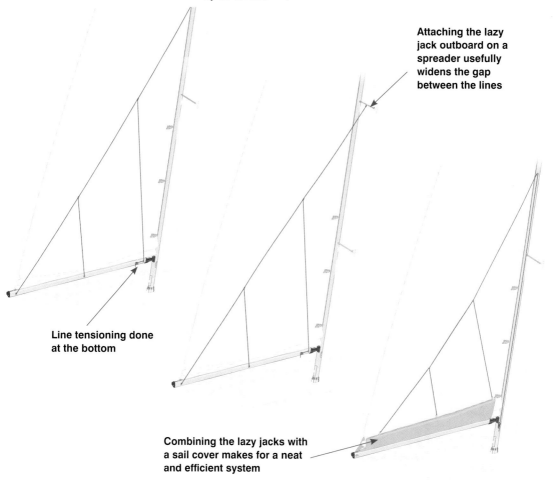

Attaching the lazy jack outboard on a spreader usefully widens the gap between the lines

Line tensioning done at the bottom

Combining the lazy jacks with a sail cover makes for a neat and efficient system

7 | Safety on deck

Having a crew member fall overboard is one of the most dangerous events that can befall a sailing yacht. To minimise the risk, every boat must make provisions to provide safety and security against this calamity.

The primary defence is a guardwire system – basically a fence around the perimeter of a deck – intended to catch anyone at risk of falling over the side.

The components of such a system are:

Pulpit and pushpit: These are fabricated rails, typically of stainless steel, fitted to a boat's bow and stern. Their height is usually determined by the stanchions – the pulpit and pushpit being the same or a little higher.

Stanchions: These are vertical posts, typically of stainless steel, either bolted to the deck or fitted into socket-type bases, also securely through-bolted.

The stanchions should be of regular height and a minimum of 2ft (0.61m) high. The spaces between stanchions – and between the pulpit, pushpit and the nearest stanchion – must not be more than 7ft (2.13m).

To complete the 'fence', the stanchions and rails are rigged with stainless steel guardwires – usually a pair of them on each side. The top wire should ideally be a minimum diameter of 5mm and is often PVC covered to reduce chafe and make it slightly

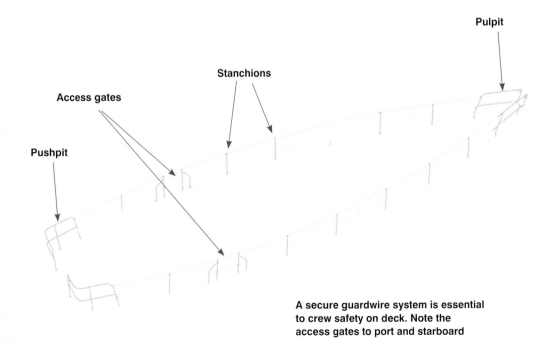

Pulpit

Stanchions

Access gates

Pushpit

A secure guardwire system is essential to crew safety on deck. Note the access gates to port and starboard

Tip You will often find stanchions fitted secured into their bases with split pins. This is a poor idea, since they will act like meat hooks, catching sails, feet and hands, if crawling along the deck. A much better arrangement is either to drill and tap and put a screw inside or have a through-bolt with a dome-headed nut. Either will make the stanchion bases cleaner, tidier and safer.

more visible in the dark. The lower wire is usually 4mm, though on larger yachts this could increase. Tensioning the guardwires can be done either by using rigging screws or lashings, with the lashings being no longer than 10cm. If rigging screws are used, they should be on the after end of the guardwires and have swaged studs rather than self-fit terminals. This will allow you to un-reave the wire through the stanchion eyes should you want to, perhaps to replace it if it becomes damaged.

The forward ends are usually attached to the pulpit using fork terminals. But there's a better way of doing it. This involves using

Split rings are potentially dangerous. This one was probably snagged and deformed by the foresheet

an eye terminal and a stainless steel 'quick link', so at the bow you will have no shackle pins or split pins that will need taping to prevent damage to sails or human skin.

Most larger yachts will have gangway stanchions that will allow you to pass through to gain access to the dinghy or quayside. Where there are gates the stanchions are braced so that when the gate pelican hook is released the rest of the guardrail wires remain taut.

One thing that I see on many yachts are split rings. These cause a lot of havoc. They can get caught on sheets or sails, which will allow the split ring to open and fall out. I notice lots of sailors use these on guard rails, pushpit and pulpit ends. They should be taped for security. Better still, they should be replaced with split pins and then taped over.

Jackstays

These are another important safety feature that allow crew members to move forward or aft when moving along the length of the vessel. It's generally recommended that jackstays be kept close to the centre line of the vessel so that you don't end up near the edge of the boat. It's not a bad idea also to fit jackstays within the confines of the cockpit.

Jackstays

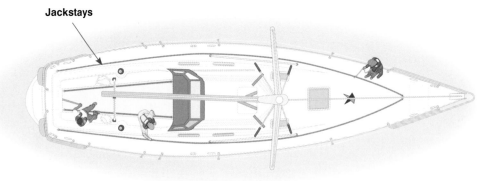

Jackstays can be made from flat polyester tape. Three-tonne breaking strain is best, though some suppliers settle for two-tonne. The ends are normally stitched into loops and they will be fitted to strong points on the deck by either shackles or lashings. You have to be aware that tape jackstays tend to degrade in sunlight – particularly the stitching that forms the eyes.

Many people have a preference for making jackstays in wire, which gives great strength, less stretch and is immune to UV damage. However, they do have a tendency to roll underfoot if trodden on.

Whatever type of jackstay you choose, there's no point in having them unless they are secured to fittings of great strength.

If they run down the side decks (a very common arrangement) crew will usually clip themselves to whichever side is to windward.

Boom Preventer

Offshore sailors like to rig preventer lines, which will prevent the boom gybing when it is payed off – typically when running off the wind.

The preventer can remain permanently attached to the outboard end of the boom. When not required, the bitter end can be taken forward to the mast, allowing a couple of metres or so of extra length, and either secured to a cleat or tied around the mast itself.

To deploy it, you simply untie it from the mast and secure the end to a foreguy.

Tip A secondary use of the preventer line occurs when going to windward. Having it rigged under the boom means it can be used as a jackstay so that you can be clipped on quite safely if you need to go forward to the mast.

When not in use this red portion of the preventer stows under the boom

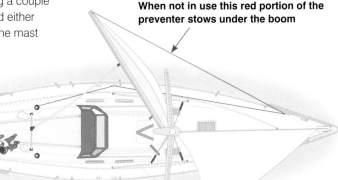

8 | Marlinspike seamanship

Important phrases:

- **'Bight'** – an open loop in a rope or chain.

- **'Bitter end'** – the secured end of a rope or chain. The inboard end of an anchor rode would be a good example.

- **'Hauling part'** – self-explanatory. The part you pull, say, on a tackle.

- **'Standing part'** – the permanently secured part of a tackle.

The word 'rope' can also cause confusion since it is used generically. Here are some more specific definitions:

- **Cord:** A small laid-up rope less than about 8mm diameter, anywhere between twine and rope.

- **Rope:** Any cordage with a diameter greater than 8mm and less than 40mm. Ropes can be made of fibres both natural and synthetic, and of wire.

- **Hawser:** Anything bigger than 40mm diameter and about as far as we need go, even on a superyacht. Not of much concern to recreational sailors.

Whippings

With synthetic ropes, it's tempting just to seal the cut ends with a hot-knife or simply an open flame, but this is rarely sufficient on its own. A conscientious sailor, however, would insist that all rope ends also be whipped and there are various ways of doing this.

Palm and Needle Whipping

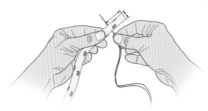

STEP 1: Thread your needle so that you have 60–70cm of double thread.

STEP 2: Push the needle into the rope end at about two and a half times the rope diameter from the bitter end. Pull the twine through the rope until you have around 10cm of end.

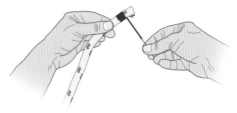

STEP 3: Now you whip the rope by rotating over the tail end towards the bitter end. For neatness, make the whipping equal to the diameter of the rope.

STEP 4: You now put the needle through the rope and out the other side. Pull tight.

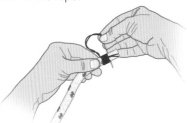

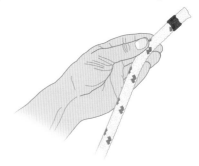

STEP 5: Now go back down to where you started and put the needle back through the rope again. Go back up to the bitter end where you will put the needle back in the rope.

STEP 6: Cut off loose ends.

NB: The best whipping twine to use is a waxed polyester at very little extra cost. It does not rot and will give many years of longevity. It also makes all the rope ends look seamanlike.

Another form of this whipping is to stitch a bale loop, and this will be used on halyard tails, reefing line tails and anywhere where you need to load or unload the mast or booms with internal or external halyards.

Left to right: messenger, lashing, bale loop and halyard

Common Whipping

STEP 1: This is where a loop is placed on the rope end and the whipping twine will be whipped onto the loop.

STEP 2: When you get the correct length of whipping you pass the whipping twine through the loop and pull the bitter end, which will bring the loop inside the whipping, trapping the bitter end. Cut off the ends. This is just used to stop rope ends from fraying.

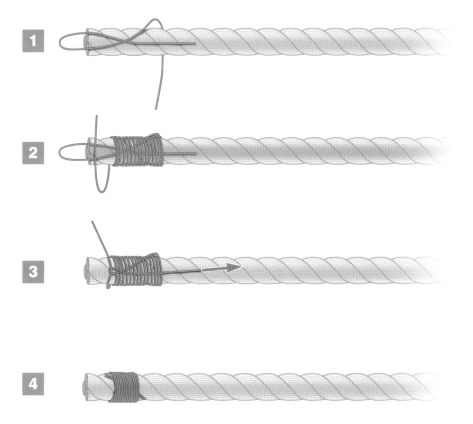

Splices

An Eye Splice in Three-strand Rope

STEP 1: Put a common whipping 30cm down from the bitter end of the rope, unravel the strands, decide on the size of the eye required, lay the strands on to the standing part.

STEP 2: Now tuck the middle strand under the top strands of the standing part from right to left. The left strand now tucks from right to left under the next strand. The third splicing strand is tucked under the strand on the standing part. You have now completed the first tuck. You will now do four more tucks to complete the splice. Cut off all loose ends and your eye splice is now finished. These are handy as a large loop to go over a bollard on the quayside or as a small loop if used to splice into an anchor chain.

Braid on Braid Eye Splice

To form an eye is a very simple procedure.

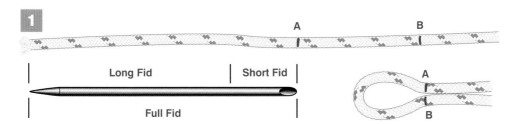

STEP 1: Put a stopper knot about 2.5 metres in the line. This will restrict any slippage between cover and core. Cut off any heat seal and milk the cover down over the core. Using the right size fid as a guide, mark point A as shown. Then form a loop to the size of eye required and mark point B.

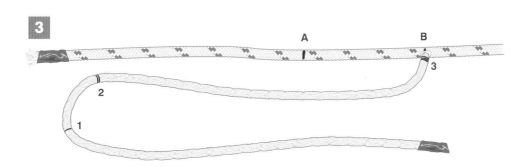

STEP 2: Next, take a smaller fid, tease open the cover's strands and extract the core at point B. Mark the core where it emerges. Tape the ends of both cover and core – which we will call 'mark 1'.

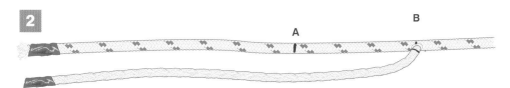

STEP 3: Pull out more core and, from mark 1, measure one short fid length. This is mark 2. Then pull out yet more core and, from mark 2, measure one full fid and one short fid length. This is mark 3.

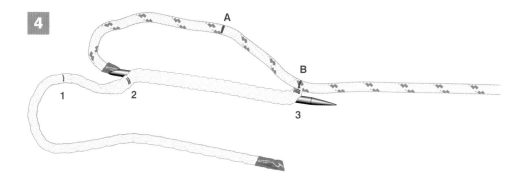

STEP 4: Place the end of the cover into the fid and insert the fid into the core at mark 2, emerging at mark 3. Pull the cover through.

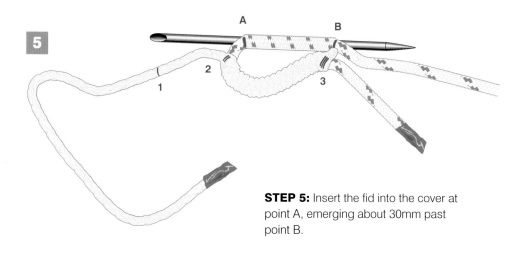

STEP 5: Insert the fid into the cover at point A, emerging about 30mm past point B.

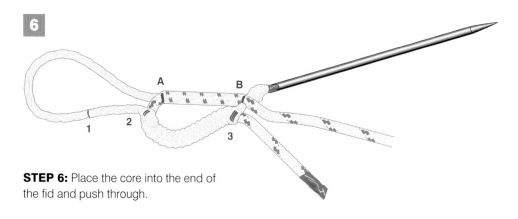

STEP 6: Place the core into the end of the fid and push through.

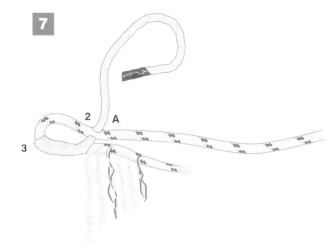

STEP 7: Pull the core through until mark 2 coincides with point A. This is the crossover point. The next task is to taper the protruding cover by pulling it out a bit and cutting off six strands as shown.

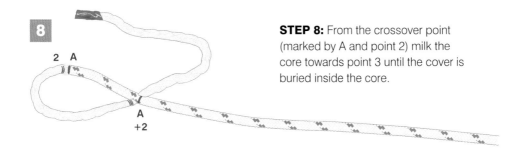

STEP 8: From the crossover point (marked by A and point 2) milk the core towards point 3 until the cover is buried inside the core.

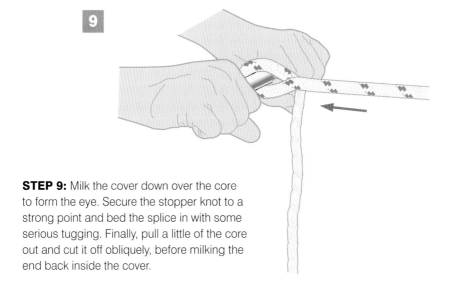

STEP 9: Milk the cover down over the core to form the eye. Secure the stopper knot to a strong point and bed the splice in with some serious tugging. Finally, pull a little of the core out and cut it off obliquely, before milking the end back inside the cover.

A Continuous Splice

Continuous line controls are becoming increasingly common. Popular uses include reefing lines, furling in-mast reefing and code zeros, and also for controlling the heights of the inboard ends of spinnaker poles.

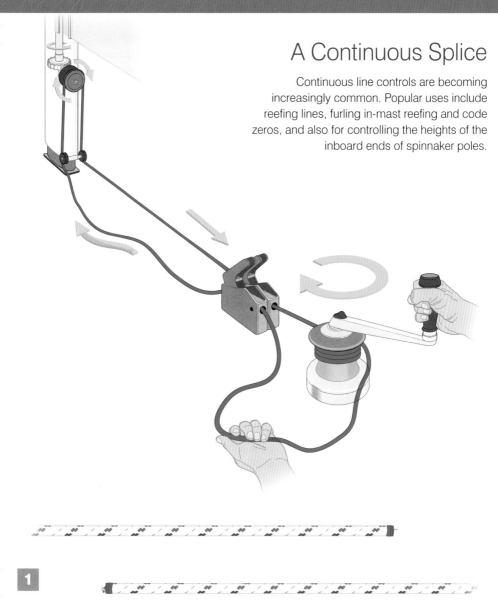

1

STEP 1: Put a palm and needle whipping 1.5 metres back from each bitter end. Also, put a light tape around both ends.

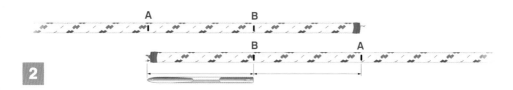

2

STEP 2: Using the appropriate size fid as a guide, mark the rope at one fid length from each bitter end, then again at two fid lengths. Let's call the marks A and B.

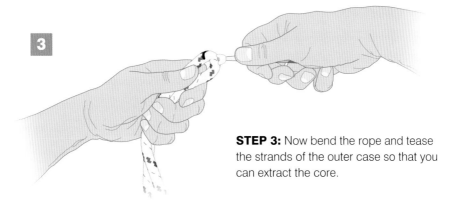

STEP 3: Now bend the rope and tease the strands of the outer case so that you can extract the core.

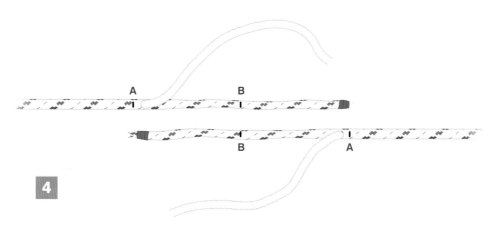

STEP 4: Enter your fid into mark B and use it to pull the cover through so it exits at mark A. Then do the same with the other outer cover so it looks like below. You now have each of the two cases inside each other.

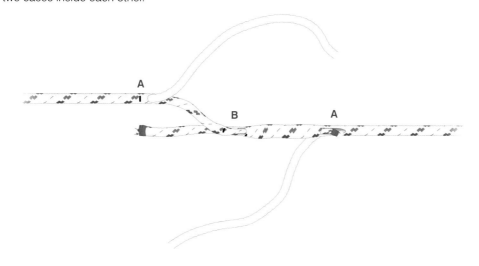

5

STEP 5: With both covers inside each other you can pull them in opposite directions to get a good 'marry'. With that done, you should tease out the exposed core.

6

STEP 6: Smooth down both interconnected covers and put a needle-and-palm whipping about 5cm each side of the marry.

7

STEP 7: The next job is to bury the core back into the rope. The best tool for this is a splicing needle. Draw the core strands back in at intervals so they form a taper.

Rope to Wire Splice

The combination of rope and wire will give you a low-stretch halyard at a relatively modest cost compared with some modern hi-tech ropes. The splice shown here joins a conventional braid-on-braid polyester rope to a 7 x 19 flexible wire rope.

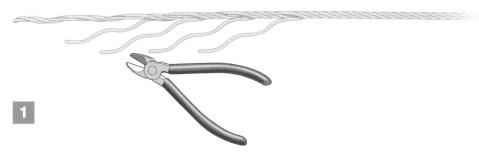

STEP 1: The object here is to taper the end of the wire over a distance of about 18cm. Start by unwinding one strand back to the 18cm mark and cut it off. Then do the same with three more successive strands, each cut off at 15cm, 12cm and 9cm respectively. This should leave you with the centre strand plus two others as shown. Tape the wire with electrical tape to cover sharp ends.

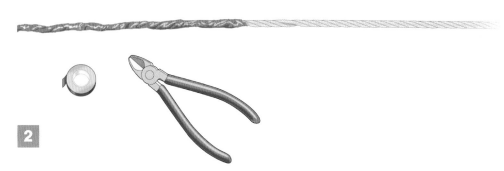

STEP 2: It's now time to prepare the rope. Start by putting a sailmaker's whipping about 2.5 metres from the bitter end. Cut off any melted end and put a light tape on the cover. Hold the end of the core and push the cover back about 60cm. It helps to put a needle temporarily through both cover and core to hold it. Cut about 20cm off the end of the core. This will later allow the cover to extend beyond the core splice.

STEP 3: Measure 40cm along the core and introduce the wire into the core using a hollow fid until it reaches the 40cm mark. Smooth the core back down onto the wire, making sure it is tight. Wrap a tape about 20cm below the end of the wire, ensuring that it is beyond the taper on an untapered part of the wire.

STEP 4: The next task involves unlaying the core and dividing it into three separate strands. Tape the ends of each strand to hold each bunch of fibres together.

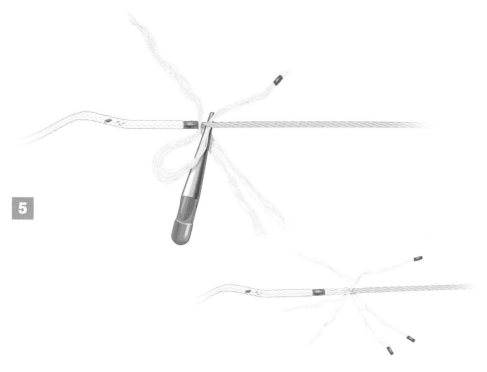

STEP 5: Now we must splice our three separate core strands into the wire, in a manner very similar to splicing three-strand rope – with the exception that each strand must pass beneath two strands of wire against the direction of the lay. A Swedish fid is an ideal tool for this job. Take five tucks, tapering after the third tuck. Trim off the ends but do not melt.

6

STEP 6: The first part of the splice is complete and all that remains is to bring the cover back down over the core splice. With the needle removed, the cover will slip down over the core splice and well beyond.

7

STEP 7: Put a common whipping over the cover at a point where the wire beneath is undistorted by the splice. Now unlay the cover back from the whipping and divide it into three strands, which must now be spliced into the wire. Unlike stage 5, this time the tucks will be made 'with the lay' – a method also known as a 'Liverpool' splice. The illustration to the right shows the Swedish fid inserted from the opposite direction to before. Again, take five full tucks and taper the next two.

8

STEP 8: A common whipping over the final taper finishes the job off neatly.

Rope to Chain Splices

Combined rope and chain anchor rodes call for special splices where the rope and chain meet. The splice in question depends on the construction of the rope. Most commonly used ropes are three-strand and octoplait (eight-strand) nylon.

Three-strand to Chain Splice

This makes use of a modified back splice in which each of the three strands pass through the last link in the chain.

1. Start by separating the strands and pushing them through the end link, two from one direction and one from the other.
2. From there, the rope is spliced in an over-and-under manner, similar to the eye splice described on page 42. Make sure you have at least seven tucks.

So as to make an easier entrance into the windlass gypsy, some riggers like to taper the splice in the following manner. After five full tucks, leave one strand behind (i.e. don't tuck it), at six tucks leave a second strand behind, and make the final tuck with only the last remaining strand. Trim off the strand ends only after all the tucks have been completed.

Octoplait to Chain Splice

For convenience's sake, I like to suspend the chain vertically with the end of the chain down-most. This gives the best access.

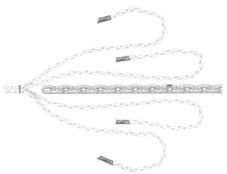

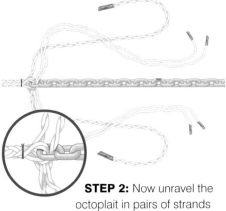

STEP 1: Mark the sixteenth link of the chain and measure the distance to the end. On the octoplait, measure one-and-a half times that length and put a sailmaker's whipping around the rope at that point.

STEP 2: Now unravel the octoplait in pairs of strands – making four pairs in all. Tape the ends of each pair to prevent fraying.

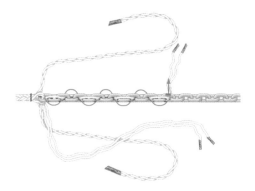

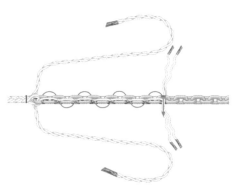

STEP 3: It's important that all pairs pass through the first link, two pairs from each direction. Pull the strands up snug.

STEP 4: From here on, pairs will pass from opposite directions, one pair through the even links and the other through the odd links, until the sixteenth link is reached.

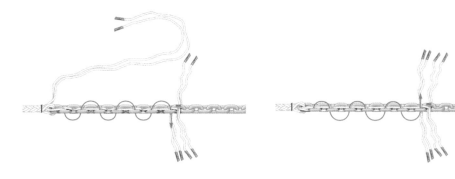

Dogged ends

STEP 5: The splice is finished by 'dogging' the strand ends together as shown above.

Knots, Bends and Hitches

The word 'knot' has come to mean a number of ways of tying ropes but the real meaning is rather more specific. Here are the generally accepted definitions:

- Knots is a word often used as a general term but, more precisely, they are used to tie a line around something – the string around a parcel of a sail tie, for instance.
- Bends are primarily intended for tying two ropes together.
- Hitches are used to tie ropes to other objects, such as rails and mooring rings.

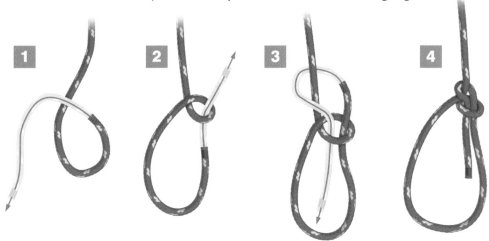

Bowline: Probably one of the most used knots on a boat. It is the quickest way to put an eye on the end of a sheet or mooring line. It is very secure and it is both easy to tie and untie. You would use this when you wanted to tie the boat up to a bollard or ring or to secure a sheet on to a sail.

A Round Turn and 2 Half Hitches: This is a very reliable and strong, easy hitch to tie. Again, you would use this if tying to a bollard or a ring on the quayside. The advantage of this particular hitch against the bowline is that it can be untied under load, unlike the bowline, which cannot be untied unless the load is released.

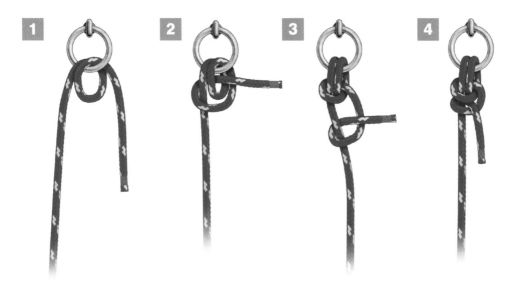

Anchor Bend or Fisherman's Bend: This is another very secure bend. It is something that you would use to tie an anchor warp to an anchor. It is made almost the same way as a round turn and 2 half hitches, but the bitter end passes under the two round turns and then is finished with two half hitches. I tend to think that this is one of the most secure bends, which will offer total security and strength to the best ability of the rope used.

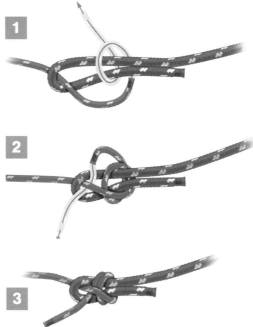

Single Sheet Bend: This is used for joining ropes of equal and unequal thicknesses. This is a very secure way of joining two lines together.

Double Sheet Bend: A double sheet bend is where the bitter end is passed with an extra turn into the eye.

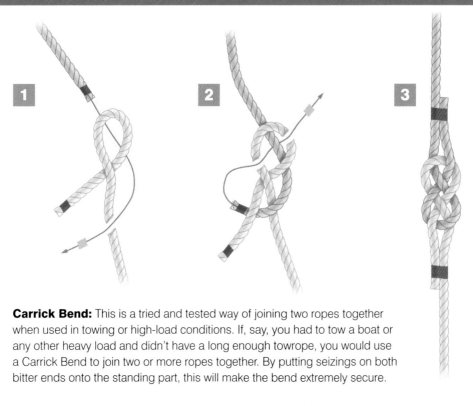

Carrick Bend: This is a tried and tested way of joining two ropes together when used in towing or high-load conditions. If, say, you had to tow a boat or any other heavy load and didn't have a long enough towrope, you would use a Carrick Bend to join two or more ropes together. By putting seizings on both bitter ends onto the standing part, this will make the bend extremely secure.

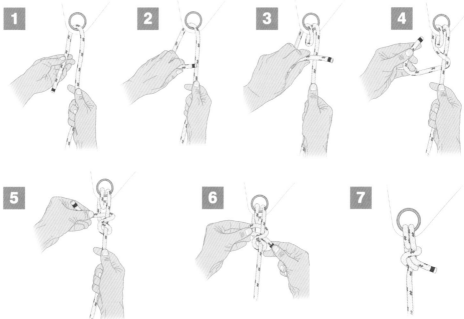

Topsail Sheet Bend: This is similar to a Round Turn and 2 Half Hitches but the two half hitches come back towards the throat of the knot to form a clove hitch and grip closely and tightly, so even if a sail is flogging heavily the bend will not come undone. This was used on sails carried high on the rigging, which could not afford to have the secured sheet become loose and fall away.

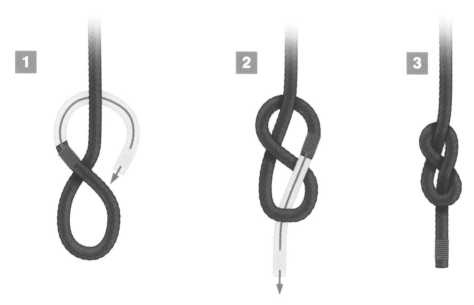

Figure-of-Eight: This is basically a stopper knot, very easy to tie, intended to prevent the end of a rope from running out through a block. Typical uses would be at the end of genoa sheets, mainsheets and halyards. Never put stopper knots on spinnaker sheets and guys because, if they have to be released quickly under extreme loads, they must be allowed to pass freely through any blocks.

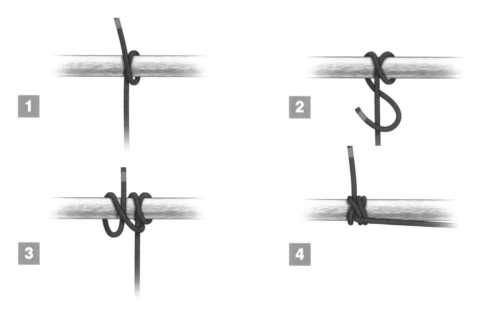

Rolling Hitch: This is usually used when you want to take the load off a sheet, guy, halyard or chain. A common application is when you get a riding turn on a winch. A short length of rope, attached with a rolling hitch, is used to transfer the load to another winch while the override is freed. It is both easy to tie and untie.

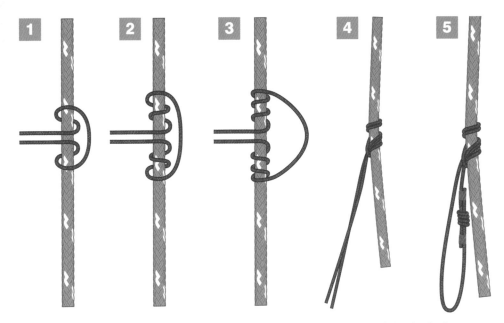

A Prusik Loop: This knot comes from the Austrian climbing community. It basically does the same job as a rolling hitch and is extremely useful when combined with a continuous rope loop.

If, say, you want to transfer a foresheet from inside the guardrails to outside the guardrails you can do so without totally relaxing the load on the sheet. The Prusik Knot is put on the sheet and the loop dropped over a convenient strong point – perhaps a nearby cleat. After sliding the knot as far as possible up the sheet, the sheet is eased a little, allowing it to be transferred to the new position. Retighten the sheet, release the loop and it's job done.

Another handy role arises when raising a headsail furling gear. The loop is attached about 1 metre down from the top end of the furling gear so that when the crane lifts it the furling drum clears the pulpit and guardrails. Once the top of the forestay is connected, you can release the halyard on the Prusik Loop, which can then be removed easily from the roller-reefing system.

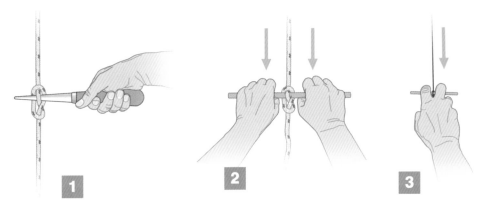

Marlinspike Hitch: This is used when you want to pull or gain leverage on a piece of rope or line. It is simple and effective to use.

Clove Hitch: This is just two half hitches onto a guardrail or any other similar object. Easy to tie and untie.

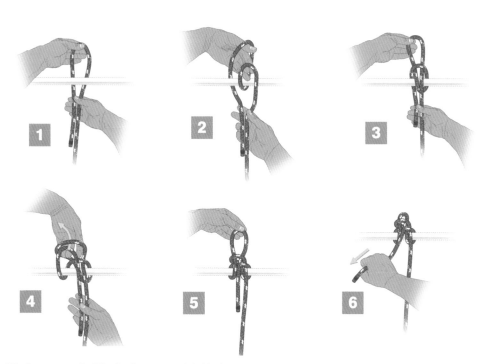

Highwayman's Hitch: Some say this hitch was used by highwaymen to release their horses in a hurry when being pursued by the law. However, for a sailor it's a useful way of temporarily securing a furled sail, enabling it to be undone in an instant. Similarly, it's useful for releasing mooring lines when shorthanded.

Lashings

Lashings are often used to secure items in position or as tensioners for such things as lifelines. They also have the advantage that in an emergency the lashing can be cut quickly to allow items to become free.

Square lashings are also used for attaching tubes or items that carry safety equipment around the pushpit area of cruising yachts. Such a lashing provides a very neat and seamanlike method of securing items to, say, the pushpit. Since there are no sharp edges, the risk of injury to the crew is greatly reduced.

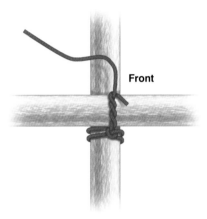

STEP 1: Start with a clove hitch and wrap the loose end around the standing part.

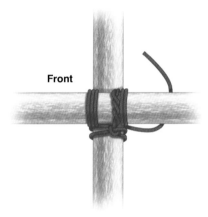

STEP 2: Take the line over the horizontal component and around the back of the vertical, down over the horizontal and behind the vertical again.

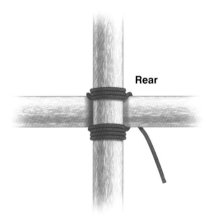

STEP 3: Repeat this circuit at least three times following the previous route.

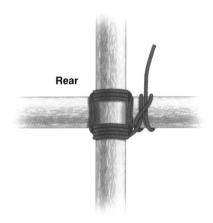

STEP 4: To tighten the wraps, apply two or three frapping turns between the two spars and finish off with a clove hitch.

Blocks and Tackles

Tackles (the phrase 'blocks and tackles' is technically incorrect) are used widely on all yachts. Examples are likely to be the main sheet, boom vangs and inside the boom for reefing lines and clew outhauls. They are used to gain mechanical advantage beyond that of which a human is capable.

The amount of this mechanical advantage is equal to the number of 'moving parts' – i.e. ropes – on the moving block. This means with two sheaves on the moving block you will have a mechanical advantage of four to one, less the inevitable losses to friction. If there are three sheaves it would give you the advantage of six to one, and so on.

Most yachts would benefit from carrying a multi-functional tackle, as shown here. This should have something like a four-to-one tackle with about two metres of rope-travel between the blocks. This tackle could be used for various applications around the boat, such as a boom preventer, lifting a dinghy or outboard, or even recovering an MOB.

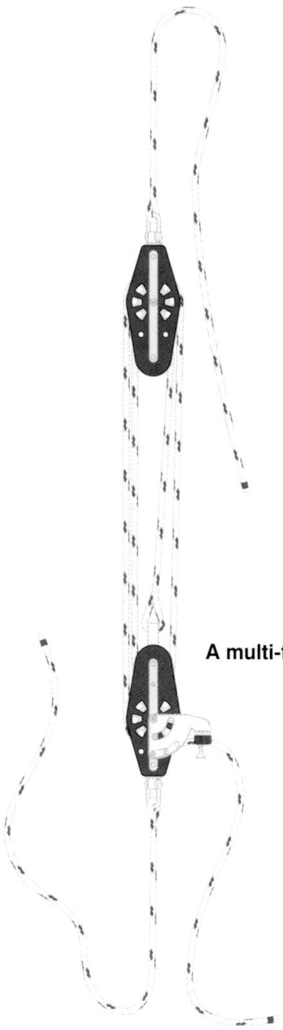

A multi-functional tackle

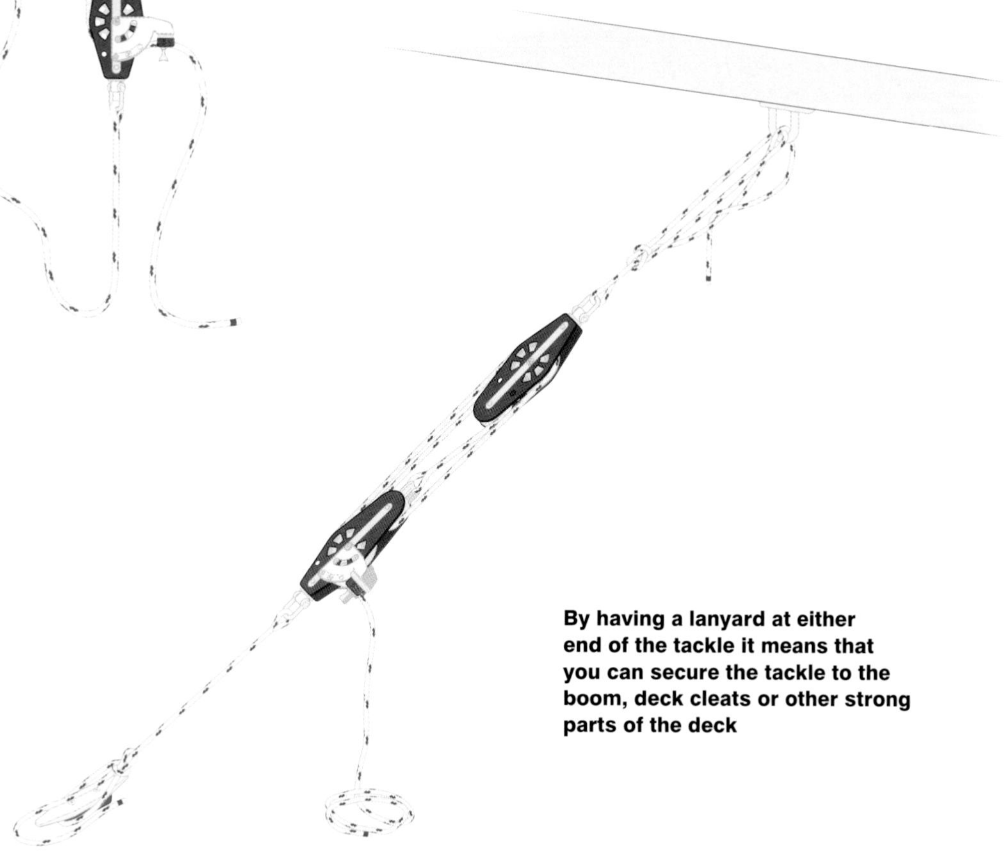

By having a lanyard at either end of the tackle it means that you can secure the tackle to the boom, deck cleats or other strong parts of the deck

Soft Shackles

Soft shackles have many uses and are becoming more and more popular. They are usually made of 12-braid HMPE (Dyneema®, Spectra®) and are strong, supple and extremely versatile. Unlike hard shackles, you can make them yourself – hence their inclusion in this chapter.

How to make a soft shackle

1

Determine the length of your soft shackle and cut your rope a few centimetres longer to allow for the stopper knot.

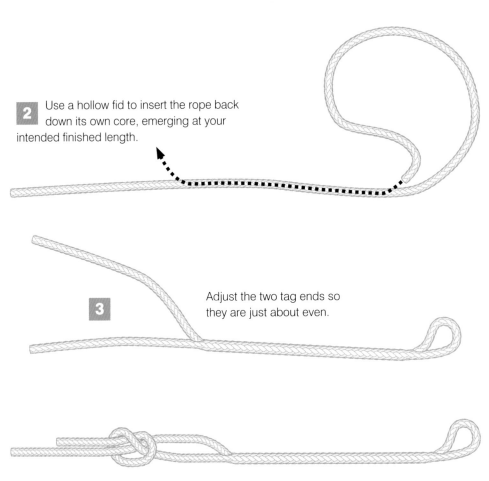

2 Use a hollow fid to insert the rope back down its own core, emerging at your intended finished length.

3 Adjust the two tag ends so they are just about even.

4 It's now time to form the stopper knot (known in the knotting world as a Matthew Walker knot). This is basically one overhand knot tied around the other end...

...followed by another tied around the first as shown.

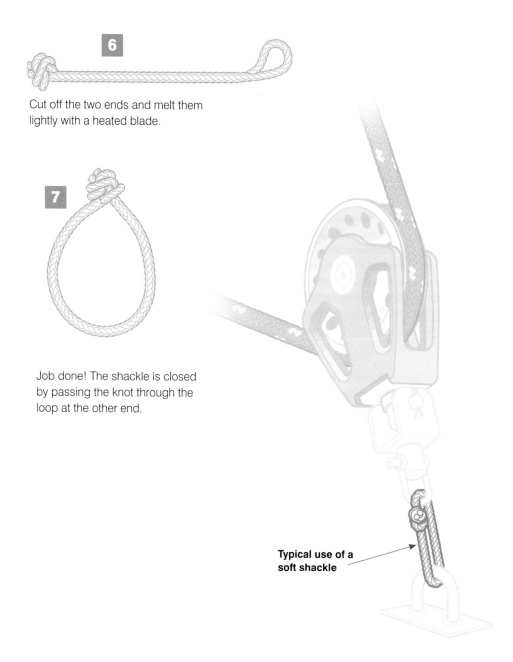

Cut off the two ends and melt them
lightly with a heated blade.

Job done! The shackle is closed
by passing the knot through the
loop at the other end.

**Typical use of a
soft shackle**

9 | Care and maintenance

Looking out for Trouble

The owner of a boat should keep a constant eye over every part of the deck, sailing gear, mast, sails and rigging. Even though you might imagine that stainless steel terminals, wire, rigging screws and shackles are seemingly indestructible, over a period of time they will suffer from the effects of load fatigue, corrosion and abrasion. Often the signs are not obvious.

Masts

Although the boom and spinnaker poles can be inspected from ground level, most of the mast towers aloft and can only be seen from a distance – unless, of course, you are prepared to climb it.

This means that for a proper inspection it is best to have it taken down so that you can inspect it closely. After a year of really hard sailing the mast would be due for a ground-level inspection. For a normal cruising boat every five years will suffice.

Then:

- Examine the mast along its length, making sure the extrusion is in good condition.

- Check the heel fitting – often an aluminium casting. Corrosion between it and the mast extrusion can expand enough to crack the extrusion. This can be saved by removing the heel fitting and cutting a few centimetres off the mast

The foot of a mast is a common site for corrosion

extrusion. The heel fitting can be cleaned up and refitted. You must then raise the mast foot fitting to the same height that you had before you cut off the mast. A teak pad will do. This will maintain your rigging lengths and height of mast.

- Check for other areas of galvanic corrosion, which can occur where

It's hard to believe these were once the ends of a pair of spreaders

dissimilar metals are in contact. Originally, any contacting areas will almost certainly have been insulated with zinc chromate or barium chromate paste, but this may have broken down over the years. Removal and reinsulating is the remedy.

Corrosion can also be found between Monel® rivets and stainless steel fittings.

■ Look out for loose fittings or those that are strained and show signs of pulling away. Spreader sockets are especially vulnerable, often levered downwards by drooping spreaders. Take a look at the outboard end of the spreaders too.

■ Also make sure the gooseneck is secure and that any wear is within

Goosenecks often combine different metals. Wear and corrosion are common

acceptable limits. If wear is severe, the whole gooseneck assembly might need replacement.

■ Check the masthead assembly with its tangs and sheaves. Make sure the sheaves turn freely and have not worn excessively. If they have, replace with new.

This cracked masthead tang was found just before a couple set off for New Zealand

No doubt what's wrong with this masthead sheave. The centre hole was once just 10mm in diameter

■ Finally, examine all electrical connections and make certain that the insulation to the various wires is still sound. Masts live in a hostile environment and wiring faults are quite common.

Booms and Spinnaker Poles

Many of the check points that apply to masts are also relevant for booms and poles, with the following additions:

■ With booms, take a close look at the mainsheet and kicker attachment fittings.

■ Most poles have some sort of latching arrangement to allow them to attach onto the mast at one end and the sail at the other. Make sure that these move freely and latch securely.

Many cruising sailors only rarely use their spinnakers. Pole ends can suffer from neglect

Standing Rigging

Except for a few types of boats that have unstayed masts, the vast majority rely on their standing rigging to hold their masts upright. And, since it only takes the failure of one single component to see the whole lot come crashing down, clearly we need to do all that we can to make sure everything is secure.

The various components are subjected to cyclic loadings. For example, all the shrouds on the windward side will be gainfully employed holding the mast to windward while the leeward rigging will be under little or no load. Then, when the boat goes about, the roles are reversed. In structural terms, this is a demanding situation that takes its toll on highly stressed components. After a while it is almost inevitable that things will start to fail.

Luckily, there are often warning signs.

■ The first thing to do is to examine every wire along its entire length, looking for broken strands. Actually, 1 x 19 wire rarely breaks in the middle of a long

Wire strands often fail where they emerge from a terminal

The crack in this T terminal would have been difficult to spot when fitted to the mast

span. The problems usually arise at areas of stress concentration, such as where the wire passes over a spreader tip or where it emerges from a swaged or self-fit terminal.

You may need to flex the wire slightly to spring a broken strand loose. Particularly at the terminals, a strand can break and remain in position – almost invisible to the casual glance unless you dislodge it.

WARNING!

Never use the standing rigging for other purposes. Some skippers like to clamp various fittings onto the wire but this is unwise because fittings tend to rub into the stainless steel wire and can crush and damage the strands.

Even worse, I have seen people tie their boats up alongside using the standing rigging! All it would take is a bit of a surge to deform and ruin the rigging screws.

The forestay is one of the hardest-working wires on a sailing boat – particularly those carrying roller-reefing gears. The most common trouble spot is at the masthead and happens when 'halyard wraps' grab the top swivel and get tangled around the top of the forestay. This can cause the wire to 'birds nest' (unwind) the lay, possibly breaking strands and seriously damaging the forestay.

Another source of trouble is the bearings inside the foil, which can produce stress concentrations and cause abrasion damage to the wire.

It is very important that the forestay is checked on a regular basis and, if the mast is down for its regular check-up, it is worth considering whether to have the forestay replaced at the same time.

This forestay was destroyed when a halyard wrapped around it

Sometimes you will notice a rogue strand that appears to be discoloured running along the lay of the wire. This dates from when the wire was manufactured and is due to the strand not being polished properly. It is no cause for concern.

Insurance companies are understandably wary of possible rig failures. Some require the standing rigging be replaced every 10 years. More commonly, insurers will ask for a full rig survey after 10 years.

Rigging Screws

Up until twenty or so years ago, most rigging screws were fabricated entirely from stainless steel. Unfortunately, these proved susceptible to 'galling' – a form of cold-welding that can irreversibly fuse the threaded components together.

Since then things have changed. Modern rigging screws retain their stainless steel threaded studs but their bodies are now made of chromed bronze. The combination of stainless steel and bronze is inherently resistant to galling.

It was also once the practice for toggles to be independent items. These days, most rigging screws come with integral toggles at their lower ends. Both are very positive developments.

Caring for rigging screws is a simple matter:

■ Make sure that the threads are clean and undamaged. If, say, a stud is bent, you can probably buy a replacement stud without the need to replace the whole rigging screw.

■ Take the rigging screw apart and clean it thoroughly. An old toothbrush and some white spirit will remove old grease and grime.

■ Lightly lubricate the bits before reassembling. Petroleum jelly (Vaseline) or Teflon® grease are good choices.

Snap Shackles

These are commonly used to secure halyards, spinnaker sheets and guys. The best-quality snap shackles are of 17-4PH electro-polished stainless steel. They are also made in titanium, which is strong, light and very expensive. All snap shackles have hinge pins and springs that need to be rinsed and oiled to be maintained in efficient working order.

Blocks

Some blocks can be dismantled for servicing but most cannot. This limits what you can do:

■ Wash blocks regularly in hot, soapy fresh water to get rid of any salt deposits. They may need lubricating, for which I would recommend light silicone or Teflon® spray.

■ The spring plungers on car-mounted blocks (such as mainsheet and genoa sheet blocks) can also be seized by salt crystals. Again, use the warm water trick and, once dry, give them a little squirt of a silicone or Teflon lubricant.

Winches

These need regular servicing. They carry very high loads and have lots of delicate moving parts internally. If the winch is sluggish or you can't turn it with your thumb, then the winch will have to be stripped down in its entirety.

Since not all winches strip down in the same way, you need the manufacturer's instructions for your particular type or model. If you don't already have them you will probably be able to download them from the internet.

But the principles are common to all winches. The object is to dismantle the winch to the point when every component can be cleaned and lightly lubricated before reassembly. Use a special winch grease – preferably the manufacturer's own – that won't emulsify and harden when doused in salt water.

> ## WARNING!
>
> **Never over-grease a winch. If applied thickly, salt water will convert even the most water-resistant grease into a dry, hard soap-like substance that will stop pawls and bearings from operating smoothly.**

To polish the winch drums, whether they be stainless steel, chrome bronze or plain bronze, just use a very light metal polish and they should shine up brightly. On aluminium winch drums just lightly spray with WD40® or similar and wipe away excess oil.

> **Tip**
>
> **If the winch is on a cockpit coaming, I always hang a piece of canvas near the winch to catch the parts before they bounce on the side deck and go into the water!**

Running Rigging

Care and attention must be paid to running rigging. Halyards will experience wear from masthead sheaves, deck turning blocks and the now often-used rope clutches. Sheets and guys will experience friction wear rubbing over guardrails or around the standing rigging. Particular attention must be paid to having fairleads so that the rope does not chafe on turning blocks or through the ends of spinnaker poles, etc. Again, the biggest predator to the life of your running rigging is sun and salt water. Sunshine actually degrades the chemical structure of the rope's construction. At the end of the season it is beneficial to check for wear and tear and wash all running rigging to take away the offending dirt and salt content. Soak the rigging in warm, fresh soapy water. Agitate it with your hands or feet or put it in the washing machine on a low temperature. This will give you a more effective usage and lifespan of your running rigging.

10 | Tools of the rigger's trade

Most yachts carry a comprehensive tool kit, which will cater for general onboard repairs and servicing. Some will be multi-purpose tools that will be useful for various tasks. Others will be more specific – serving only a single purpose.

Here I'm assuming that you will already have shipped some large adjustable spanners and heavy screwdrivers that can be used as pry bars when it comes to tensioning the rigging.

The tools listed below are the specialised ones you will need for working with rope and wire.

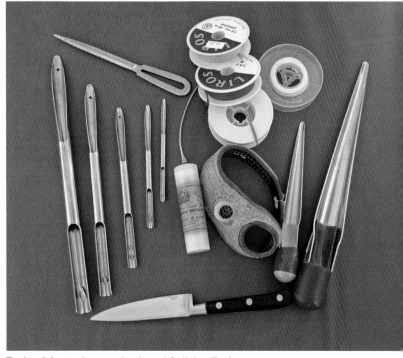

Tools of the trade – a selection of Splicing Tools

Knife: A good knife with a blade of a generous length, say 12–15cm, is absolutely essential. It must be as sharp as can reasonably be achieved, since a blunt knife is both dangerous and useless. So, along with the knife, you should have a good sharpening stone.

Marlinspikes: These are normally made of steel – often stainless – and are used for splicing three-strand rope and wire.

A Swedish Fid: This is a very useful tool. It is made in stainless steel and has a hollow section, so that when the fid is inserted into the rope it allows a gap for the strand to pass through easily.

Splicing spikes or fids are used for splicing braided ropes. You will also need to complement the spikes with a pusher. As the splicing fid is passed into the rope the pusher will push the strands into the plaited rope. Pushers are usually made of steel.

Norwegian Fids: This is an economical, very effective set of splicing needle fids. These are hollow and also have a little pin within the hollow needle so that you can put your rope through and pull the needle through the braided line.

Splicing Needles: Also used for splicing braided rope. They are made of steel, are approximately 30cm long and about 5mm in diameter, with a flattened end and an elongated hole so that the strands of the case or core of the rope can be threaded inside a plaited rope. We use various types of fids and splicing needles according to the manufacture and construction of the plaited ropes.

A Sailmaker's Palm: Without this useful tool it would be very difficult to push a needle through a heavy rope or layers of canvas. Palms are usually made of leather and have a small steel disc in the palm of the hand with which to push the needle. Some are adjustable to fit various hand sizes but the professionals tailor their palms to fit themselves alone. Either way, it pays to buy a good one.

Sailmakers' Needles: These specialist needles have a triangular section to push obstinate strands aside. They come in a wide range of sizes and it's a good idea to carry an assortment. They are used for stitching (sail repairs being a typical task) and, of course, for doing a 'palm and needle' whipping.

Whipping Twine: This comes in a number of different thicknesses. Carry as large

a selection as you possibly can as you never know what you are going to need it for. Whipping twine is available unwaxed or waxed, with the latter being a little more expensive but more versatile.

Other tools that would be useful are:
- Pliers and/or vice grips.
- Wire cutters.
- Tape measure.

- Gas-fired hot knife for cutting and sealing the ends of synthetic ropes.
- Adhesive tape – mainly electrical type. Carry an assortment of tapes if possible for multipurpose use.

In all my years of sailing the Atlantic, Europe, Caribbean and Mediterranean I have been extremely lucky never to have experienced a dismasting.

However, such calamities can happen, so for anyone going offshore it's essential that every boat carries the gear necessary to cut any wreckage loose before it can stove a hole in the hull side.

The best tools for this are:
- Heavy-duty bolt cropper to cut the rigging screws and…
- heavy duty wire cutter to sever the wire. Note that these two tools are not the same thing!

Tip Cutting Wire

If you don't have a proper wire cutter the wire can be cut with a hacksaw. Tape the wire at its cutting point, and put two pieces of wooden cleating nailed to a piece of ply round it. The wire is now entrapped. Then cut through the cleating and wire and you will have a very clean cut. Lubricate the cutting blade.

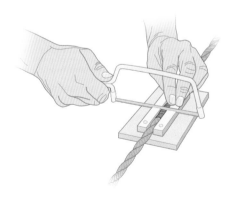

11 | Preparing for a voyage

There's more to preparing for an offshore voyage than simply loading stores aboard. When away from land you must be prepared for any eventuality. Of course, you can even be caught out in home waters, but the farther you sail offshore the more self-reliant you must be.

Before setting off you should either go up the mast or send someone to the top to check over all the main rigging attachment points. At the risk of repetition you should:

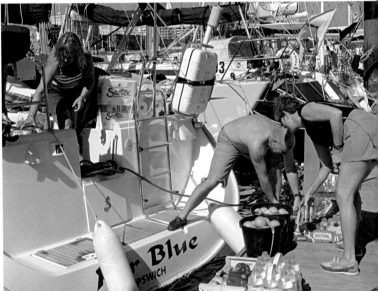

- Make sure that all the sheaves are in good working order and that the spinnaker and external blocks are in sound condition.
- Any shackles or pins should be wired to prevent them coming loose.
- Attention should be given to the top end of the roller furling system.
- Also to be checked is the security of the spreaders, both the inboard ends that are attached to the mast and the outboard ends that the standing rigging passes through or is attached to. Also needed would be spreader tip protection, which will aid against damage to the sails.
- Whilst up the mast you will have to check the lights, aerials, VHF and antennas. Bulbs can be checked in lights, aerials can be secured, and check that there are no abrasions on cable insulations.
- Radar brackets, radar reflectors and steaming lights also deserve attention.

Make sure that no halyards come in contact with electronic equipment.

- All the rigging attachments at deck level must be carefully inspected so that rigging screws are locked and won't vibrate loose and that all sharp split pins will not cut either the sheets or the crew's hands or oilskins.
- If the mast is deck stepped you must protect the cables that are coming out of the base of the mast. These are prone to damage while working around the mast area.
- Don't forget to make sure that all ancillary deck gear – anchor, spinnaker poles and anything fastened to the deck – must be securely attached or otherwise they could be washed away when heavy seas are breaking over the deck.

Appendix

Stainless Steel Wire

Made from high tensile stainless steel wire 316 specification.

1 x 19

This form of construction is used for making standing rigging, guardrails etc. It is made by winding six strands around a central strand, then 12 strands around those six inner strands – making 19 in total. All the strands are the same diameter. It has low stretch properties but isn't very flexible.

Diameter (mm)	Breaking Strain (kg)
2	315
2.5	495
3	715
4	1275
5	1950
6	2850
7	3525
8	4630
10	7240
12	10300
14	14170
16	18550

Roller swaged or self-fit end fittings are invariably used for this type.

Dyform® (or Compaque®) 1 x 19

This form of 1 x 19 wire uses shaped outer strands in order to include more material within any given diameter. This means you get greater strength and less stretch (also less 'windage') and makes it a popular choice for performance yachts. Unsurprisingly, it costs more than regular 1 x 19 wire.

Diameter (mm)	Breaking Strain (kg)
5	2430
6	3540
7	4906
8	6140
10	9760
12	14350
14	19250

Roller swaged or self-fit end fittings are invariably used for this type.

7 x 19 Stainless Steel Wire

7 x 19 wire is the first choice when flexibility is an asset. It's used for such things as halyards, lift wires on davits and also steering cables on yachts with wheel steering. The wire is constructed with one central core comprising 19 wires, then six strands, each also of 19 wires, wound around the core. So for the given diameter you will have a total of 133 wires.

Predictably, for any given diameter 7 x 19 is not as strong as 1 x 19.

Diameter (mm)	Breaking Strain (kg)
2	225
3	500
4	900
5	1400
6	2030
7	2750
8	3620
10	5670

As with the other wires, it's possible to use a wide variety of end fittings. However, it is more usual to fit a Talurit® swage fitting where the wire is put around a thimble and a copper sleeve is hydraulically clamped. This produces an eye in which to put a shackle or link.

Comparisons between these three types can be seen by studying the graph below.

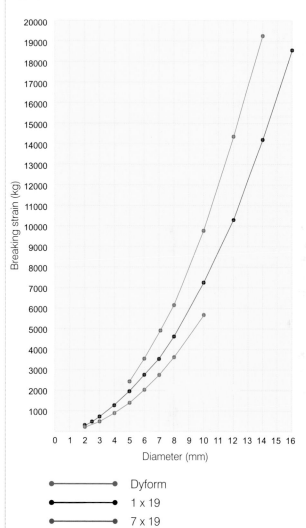

Dyform
1 x 19
7 x 19

Tapping guide for aluminium

Thread Size	Tapping Drill Size
3mm	2.4mm
4mm	3.25mm
5mm	4.0mm
6mm	5.0mm
8mm	6.8mm
10mm	8.5mm

Ropes

As we have seen in the preceding pages, ropes play a vital part in life afloat, acting as control lines for the sails, mooring lines when alongside, and serving a host of other functions.

They come in a variety of materials, some exotic and others that are commonplace or are becoming commonplace as their qualities are more fully appreciated.

Let's look at the physical properties of some examples.

Polyester

This workhorse of the marine cordage world comes in a variety of different constructions but the most common is known as braid-on-braid, which, as the name suggests, means a braided core that is shrouded by a braided cover.

All in all it is an excellent general-purpose rope, having tolerably low stretch and a fair degree of UV resistance. A little tricky to splice, but a little practice brings mastery.

Diameter (mm)	Breaking Strength (kg)
6	1350
8	2000
10	3150
12	4300
14	6000
16	7250
18	8500
20	11000

Three-strand Polyester

Easier to splice than braid-on-braid. Used on many traditional yachts where braided ropes might look out of place.

Diameter (mm)	Breaking Strength (kg)
6	1300
8	1700
10	2580
12	3350
14	4100
16	5400
18	6400
20	7300
24	10000

High Modulus Polyethylene (Dyneema®, Spectra®)

A cruising version of this high-performance fibre is represented by Dyneema Cruising®, where an HMPE core is covered in braided polyester.

It is quite expensive but its cost can be justified on high-performance yachts anxious to save weight and windage aloft. Since HMPE is naturally resistant to UV attack, in some instances, the polyester cover can be discarded to make further weight savings.

Diameter (mm)	Breaking Strength (kg)
6	2000
8	2500
10	3500
12	4400

Three-strand Nylon

A stretchy fibre, subject to grime absorption and stiffening, nylon still remains the first choice for mooring lines and anchor warps.

Diameter (mm)	Breaking Strength (kg)
6	1090
8	1700
10	2500
12	3150
14	4700
16	6100
18	7300
20	8000

Galvanic Corrosion

As we noted back on page 11, galvanic corrosion is a constant threat to aluminium alloy masts. When two dissimilar metals are in contact or in very close proximity to each other, and immersed (or even regularly sprayed) by an electrolyte such as seawater, an electric current will be produced. And the more anodic (i.e. less noble) of that pair will be eaten away.

To illustrate this, a galvanic table of various materials (all are metals except carbon) is shown here, each in their relative positions on the galvanic scale. Of particular concern to boaters are aluminium and stainless steel – both commonly used in combination on masts and other fittings (here highlighted in yellow to make them easier to spot). The scale at the top of the table shows that the potential difference between them in volts is nearly 1 volt. Being the less noble of the pair it's the aluminium that will suffer. Had the mast been carbon fibre (graphite) the stainless steel would be under threat – but not nearly so much so since graphite and stainless steel are relatively close on the scale.

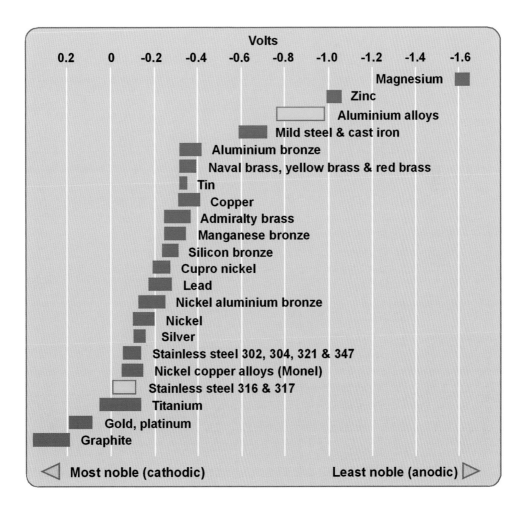